Complete Art Curriculum Activities Kit

150 Easy-to-Use Art Lessons, in 8 Exciting Creative Media for Grades 1-8

Barbara McNally Reuther
Diane Enemark Fogler

Parker Publishing Company
Paramus, New Jersey 07652

Library of Congress Cataloging-in-Publication Data

Reuther, Barbara McNally.
    [Art curriculum activities kits]
    Complete art curriculum activities kit : 150 easy-to-use art lessons in 8 exciting
media for grades 1–8 / Barbara McNally Reuther, Diane Enemark Fogler.
        p. cm.
    Originally published in 2 v. as: Art curriculum activities kits. Primary level. And Art Curriculum
activities kits. Intermediate level. West Nyack, NY : Parker Pub. Co., ©1988.
    ISBN 0-13-042552-4
    1. Art—Study and teaching—United States. 2. Activity programs in education—United States.
I. Fogler, Diane Enemark. II. Title.

N353.R48   2001
372.5'044—dc21   2001032112

Acquisitions Editor: *Win Huppuch*
Production Editor: *Jacqueline Roulette*
Layout/Interior Design: *Celestial Engineering*

Printed in the United States of America

10 9 8 7 6 5 4 3 2 1

ISBN 0-13-042552-4

Originally published as *Art Curriculum Activities Kit: Primary Level* and *Art Curriculum Activities Kit: Intermediate Level* ©1988 by Parker Publishing Company.

ATTENTION: SCHOOLS AND CORPORATIONS

PARKER PUBLISHING COMPANY
Paramus, New Jersey 07652

http://www.phdirect.com

Dedication

To my husband, Charlie,
for his enthusiastic support and encouragement,
and to my parents,
the most creative teachers I know.

B.M.R.

To the children I have taught,
who made each day
a challenge and an adventure.

D.E.F.

Acknowledgments

We wish to thank Win Huppuch for the chance he offered us to do this book, and Ann Leuthner for her editorial assistance and reassuring support throughout the original publication.

About the Authors

Barbara McNally Reuther (B.A. in Art, College of Saint Elizabeth, Convent Station, NJ) has taught art for over ten years at both the primary and the intermediate levels. At both levels, she initiated enrichment classes, which later became part of the regular school curriculum. She is currently working as a freelance illustrator and painter.

Diane Enemark Fogler (B.A. in Art & Education, Bradley University, Peoria, IL; M.A. in Art & Education, C.W. Post, Long Island University, Greenvale, NY) has taught art at the elementary, junior high school, and senior high school levels for more than thirty years. She currently teaches art at the elementary level and serves as art coordinator for conducted in-service art workshops for classroom teachers and has also worked extensively with gifted students in an art enrichment program. She has served as art director at various day camps and recreation centers and has also written her district's elementary art curriculum as well as several articles for *School Arts Magazine*.

About This Art Education Teaching Resource

Complete Art Curriculum Activities Kit gives classroom teachers and art specialists a comprehensive, sequentially organized art curriculum for students in grades 1 through 8. The curriculum provides 150 stimulating creative lessons in eight different media that teach basic and advanced art concepts and skills and meet the needs of students at various age and skill levels.

For easy use, the activities are organized into two parts: I. Art Activities for the Primary Grades and II. Art Activities for the Intermediate Grades. Each part includes eight media sections focusing on Drawing, Painting, Weaving, Color and Design, Ceramics, Paper Crafts, Printmaking, and Crafts. The activities within each media section are sequenced according to three levels of complexity, which can be used by different grade levels, depending on students' skill development.

Each lesson is complete and self-contained, including a descriptive title, a full-page illustration, list of specific materials needed, and step-by-step directions that can be easily understood by students. Both illustration and direction pages can be photocopied as many times as required for use with individual students, small groups, or an entire class. The lessons make use of inexpensive and commonly available materials and have been classroom-tested by the authors.

The organized format and clear graphic presentation make it possible for the teacher with little or no previous training or experience in art instruction to teach these lessons successfully. The art specialist will find that they offer a valuable curricular guide and ability-level sourcebook.

One of the most important features of this art activities program is the skill level sequence of the lessons in each art medium. The following examples of weaving activities provide an overview of the developmental process from Level 1 to Level 6. At each level new skills are introduced while previously acquired skills and techniques are reinforced.

About This Art Education Teaching Resource
WEAVING

PART I:
ART ACTIVITIES FOR THE PRIMARY GRADES (GR. 1-4)

LEVEL 1 LEVEL 2 LEVEL 3

PART II:
ART ACTIVITIES FOR THE INTERMEDIATE GRADES (GR. 5-8)

LEVEL 4 LEVEL 5 LEVEL 6

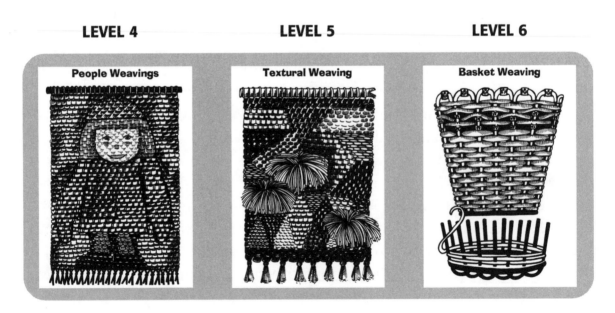

Straight Weaving · Circle Weaving · Straw Weaving

People Weavings · Textural Weaving · Basket Weaving

About This Art Education Teaching Resource

Special features of this practical resource for elementary classroom teachers and elementary and middle school art specialists include:

- A comprehensive, sequential art curriculum for grades 1–8, depending on individual ability levels

- Innovative activities in eight different art media which teach basic and advanced art skills and concepts

- 150 ready-to-use art lessons with full-page illustrations of each that can be used for demonstration purposes or to give helpful ideas on what to add to each project

- Smaller "how to" illustrations accompanying the step-by-step directions for ease of use

- Each art concept builds upon another art concept, providing a strong foundation for all future art skills

- Each lesson provides a list of specific materials needed and easy-to-follow step-by-step directions for making that project

- The Table of Contents presents the activities in two convenient forms; (1) by art media and (2) by six skill levels so that art lessons are easily located for students with varying art skills

- All activities have been classroom tested and proven effective

Using the activities in this unique resource, no teacher need be an "artist" to conduct a successful art education program. Moreover, the lessons at both primary and intermediate levels can be used in sequence to provide a complete art curriculum in themselves or be used to supplement and enrich your existing curriculum.

This Ready-to-Use Art Activities Program explores and introduces a wide variety of art forms and media, which help to build sequential art skills while reinforcing skills previously used. And each activity is fun and unique—so enjoy!

Barbara McNally Reuther
Diane Enemark Fogler

Contents

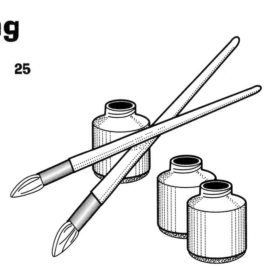

Contents

Section V: Paper Crafts

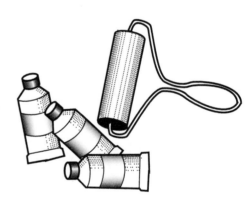

Section VI: Printmaking

Section VII: Weaving

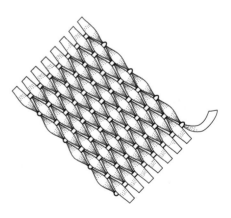

Contents

PART II:
ART ACTIVITIES FOR THE
INTERMEDIATE GRADES (Gr. 5–8)

SECTION II: Painting

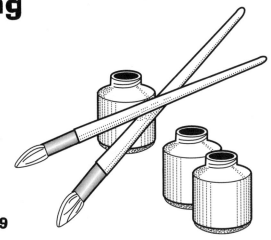

SECTION III: Color and Design

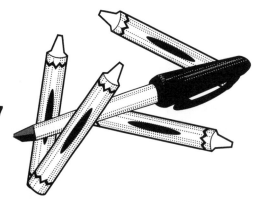

Contents

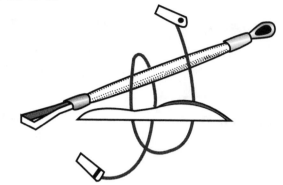

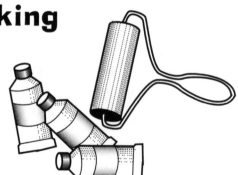

Section VII: Weaving

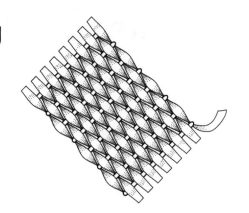

Section VIII: Crafts

PRIMARY LEVEL

Focus Areas

	line	shape	value	color	texture	perspective & proportion	pattern & composition	cultural enrichment	creative thinking
Section I: Drawing									
I-1 Self-Portrait	•	•				•		•	•
I-2 Body Portraits	•	•		•		•		•	•
I-3 Castle Drawings		•				•	•	•	•
I-4 Royal Portrait	•	•		•		•		•	•
I-5 Motivational Drawings			•		•		•		•
I-6 Hide and Seek	•	•	•		•	•	•		•
I-7 Zoo Murals		•		•	•	•			•
I-8 Scratchboards	•		•		•		•		•
I-9 Imagination Machines	•	•				•	•		•
Section II: Painting									
II-1 Giant Paper Ice Cream Cones	•	•		•			•		•
II-2 Pussy Willows	•	•	•	•	•	•			•
II-3 Sidewalk Paintings	•	•		•		•		•	•
II-4 Painted Skeletons	•	•				•		•	•
II-5 Big Bad Bug Painting	•	•		•		•	•		•
II-6 Painted Turkeys	•	•		•		•	•		•
II-7 Glowing Fish	•	•	•	•	•	•			•
II-8 Fabric Painting	•	•		•			•	•	•
Section III: Color and Design									
III-1 Letter Pictures	•	•					•		•
III-2 Horizontal and Vertical Designs	•		•	•			•		•
III-3 Crayon Picture Puzzles	•	•	•	•		•	•		•
III-4 Photograms	•	•	•				•		•
III-5 All-Over Patterns	•	•	•				•		•
III-6 One Shape Only	•	•	•				•		•
III-7 Crayon Fireworks	•	•	•	•			•		•
III-8 Pattern Birds	•	•		•	•	•			•
III-9 Line Art	•		•				•		•
III-10 Word Pictures	•	•	•	•			•		•
III-11 Sunglasses		•		•			•		•
III-12 Collage Portraits	•	•		•	•	•	•	•	•
III-13 Costume Collage		•			•	•	•		•
Section IV: Ceramics									
IV-1 Clay Candlesticks	•	•			•		•	•	•
IV-2 Ceramic Coil Mirrors	•	•			•				•
IV-3 Clay Face Necklaces		•			•	•			•
IV-4 Heart Frames and Necklaces	•	•		•	•		•		•
IV-5 Clay Bells		•		•	•		•		•
IV-6 Clay Pockets		•			•		•		•
IV-7 Coil Pottery	•	•			•		•	•	•
IV-8 Clay Appliqué Plaques	•	•		•	•		•		•
IV-9 Evergreen Plaques	•	•	•		•				•

PRIMARY LEVEL

Focus Areas

	line	shape	value	color	texture	perspective & proportion	pattern & composition	cultural enrichment	creative thinking
Section V: Paper Crafts									
V-1 Torn Paper Trees	•	•		•	•	•	•		•
V-2 Paper Bag Houses		•		•	•	•			•
V-3 Stitched Paper Puppets	•	•		•		•		•	•
V-4 Quilling Valentines	•	•			•	•	•	•	•
V-5 Paper Sculpture Animals		•		•	•	•			•
V-6 Witches	•	•		•	•	•			•
V-7 Oaktag Houses	•	•				•		•	•
V-8 Tissue Paper Fish Kites		•		•		•	•		•
V-9 Two-Cardboard Relief	•	•	•		•		•		•
V-10 Dancing Bears	•	•				•			•
V-11 Landscape in the Round	•	•							•
V-12 Lunar Shadow Boxes	•	•	•	•	•	•			•
V-13 Paper Bag People		•				•		•	•
V-14 Tissue Paper Silhouettes	•	•	•			•			•
Section VI: Printmaking									
VI-1 Handprints	•	•			•				•
VI-2 Texture Prints	•	•		•	•		•	•	•
VI-3 Chalk Prints		•	•	•			•		•
VI-4 Two-Color Styrofoam Prints	•	•	•		•		•		•
VI-5 Tempera Tile Prints	•	•	•		•		•		•
VI-6 Leaf Prints	•	•	•		•		•		•
VI-7 Gadget Prints	•	•	•	•	•		•		•
Section VII: Weaving									
VII-1 Straight Weaving	•			•	•		•	•	•
VII-2 Circle Weaving	•	•	•	•	•		•	•	•
VII-3 Paper Weaving	•	•	•	•	•		•	•	•
VII-4 Ojos de Dios	•		•	•	•		•	•	•
VII-5 Straw Weaving	•	•	•	•	•		•	•	•
Section VIII: Crafts									
VIII-1 Stuffed Butterflies		•		•		•	•		•
VIII-2 Planetary Architecture	•	•		•	•	•			•
VIII-3 Point-to-Point Yarn Designs	•	•		•			•		•
VIII-4 Soft Foam Masks	•	•		•	•			•	•
VIII-5 Constructional Problem Solving	•	•	•						•
VIII-6 Complete the Picture		•	•			•			•
VIII-7 Wood Sculpture	•	•		•	•	•	•		•
VIII-8 Hand Puppets		•		•	•	•		•	•
VIII-9 Aluminum Plaster Casting	•		•	•				•	•
VIII-10 Metal Masks	•	•		•		•			•

INTERMEDIATE LEVEL

Focus Areas

Section I: Drawing

	line	shape	value	color	texture	perspective & proportion	pattern & composition	cultural enrichment	creative thinking
I-1 Action Figures	•	•				•			•
I-2 Pen and Ink Owls	•	•	•		•	•	•	•	•
I-3 Two-Pencil Drawings	•	•	•				•		•
I-4 Musical Still Life	•	•		•		•	•	•	•
I-5 Personality Profiles	•	•	•			•	•	•	•
I-6 Window Views	•	•	•	•		•	•	•	•
I-7 Half-Face Portraits	•	•	•		•	•		•	•
I-8 Whale Dreams	•	•				•			•
I-9 Architecture in Our Town	•	•			•	•		•	•
I-10 Portraiture		•	•	•	•	•		•	•
I-11 Two-Point Perspective	•	•				•		•	•
I-12 Bicycle Drawings	•	•				•	•		•
I-13 Texture Drawings	•	•	•		•	•			•
I-14 Idiomatic Illustrations	•	•		•					•

Section II: Painting

	line	shape	value	color	texture	perspective & proportion	pattern & composition	cultural enrichment	creative thinking
II-1 Foil Clowns	•	•		•	•		•		•
II-2 Window Portraits	•	•		•	•	•			•
II-3 Jungle Resist	•	•	•	•	•		•		•
II-4 Pointillism		•	•	•			•		•
II-5 Sand Paintings		•		•	•			•	•
II-6 Warm and Cool Colors		•	•	•			•	•	•
II-7 Monochromatic Painting		•	•	•				•	•
II-8 Multimedia Slides	•	•	•	•	•		•		•

Section III: Color and Design

	line	shape	value	color	texture	perspective & proportion	pattern & composition	cultural enrichment	creative thinking
III-1 Art Object Designs	•	•	•	•			•		•
III-2 Magazine Textures	•	•	•		•	•	•		•
III-3 Paper Mosaic		•	•	•	•		•	•	•
III-4 Geometric Pictures	•	•	•	•			•		•
III-5 Rainbow Pictures	•	•					•		•
III-6 Multimedia Mosaic	•	•	•	•			•		•
III-7 Negative/Positive Designs	•	•	•				•		•
III-8 Design a Van	•	•		•		•			•
III-9 Candy Jars	•	•		•	•	•		•	•
III-10 One Line Only	•	•			•				•
III-11 Color and Design	•	•	•	•			•		•
III-12 Radial Designs	•	•	•	•			•		•
III-13 Optical Illusions	•	•	•				•		•
III-14 Lettering	•	•					•		•

INTERMEDIATE LEVEL
Focus Areas

PART I

ART ACTIVITIES FOR THE PRIMARY GRADES

Drawing

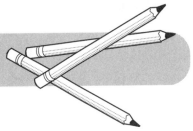

LEVEL 1

The first activity in this section introduces and explores the *Self-Portrait* and demonstrates the important role observation skills play in creating realistic drawings. *Body Portraits* is a large-as-life lesson that concentrates on the use of contour lines in figure drawings. The narrative nature of drawing is examined in *Castle Drawings,* a lesson that also introduces the technique of cross-sectioning.

LEVEL 2

The Royal Portrait is a simplified introduction to formal compositional elements. In *Motivational Drawings,* creative drawing from imagination is emphasized. *Hide and Seek* is a lesson that imaginatively demonstrates how overlapping can be used in a drawing to create the illusion of depth. It is also a lesson in developing an eye for detail. The *Zoo Mural,* which is suggested as a group project, introduces the mural as an art form and shows how found objects and other materials can be combined to create a collage.

LEVEL 3

In *Scratchboards,* different types of lines and their various characteristics are examined. *Imagination Machines* is a lesson that encourages the students to apply the same eye for detail employed in drawings from life to their drawing from imagination.

Self-Portrait

Hide and Seek

Scratchboards

Self-Portrait

Self-Portrait

MATERIALS:

- **12" x 18" white paper**
- **scissors**
- **12" x 18" black paper**
- **crayons**

DIRECTIONS:

1. Think of the three main parts of your body: your head, your trunk, and your legs.

2. Your head is connected to your trunk by your neck, which is almost as wide as your head.

3. Shoulders are on top of your trunk and are about twice as wide as your head.

4. The arms begin at the ends of the shoulders, and they can bend in half at the elbow.

5. Don't forget hands and fingers.

6. The legs begin from the bottom of the trunk and can bend in half at the knee.

7. Don't forget about feet and toes.

8. Think about your own special features: What color hair and eyes do you have? Is your hair long or short, curly or straight? Do you have bangs, or do you wear your hair tied in some way or with barrettes? Do you wear glasses?

9. What kind and color of clothes do you have on today? What about your shoes?

10. Begin to draw yourself as large as possible vertically on the white paper and remember all the items you have thought about.

11. When you have finished, cut out your picture and glue it onto black paper. Remember to squeeze the glue on the back of the white paper in a little line of glue running near the edge of the paper.

Body Portraits

Body Portraits

MATERIALS:

- **thin black marker**
- **36" x 4' piece of paper**
- **tempera paint and brushes**
- **scissors**

DIRECTIONS:

1. Lay paper on floor or table.

2. Lay down on the paper and assume any position you want. Try to have your arms and legs separated, but do not lay them across your body.

3. Have someone trace slowly and completely around you with a marker showing your complete outline.

4. Get up and complete the "inside" of the drawing, adding lines for clothes and shoes, a face, and a line where the hair surrounds the face.

5. Paint in with tempera.

6. When dry, cut out.

Castle Drawings

Castle Drawings

MATERIALS:

- 12" x 18" white drawing paper
- pencil and eraser
- thin black marker

DIRECTIONS:

1. Think of what the back of a doll house looks like—all open so that you can see into all the rooms at the same time. This is called a cross-section.

2. Think of what a castle looks like—walls, towers, battlements, gateways, an interior with stairs.

3. Draw a castle this same way showing all the rooms: a banquet hall and kitchen, a dungeon, the throne room, some bedrooms, an entrance hall, and any other type of room you may think would have been found in a castle.

4. Add people doing various jobs in all the rooms to make the castle life run smoothly.

5. Add furniture, rugs, or banners hanging on the walls, and swords and shields for decorations.

Royal Portrait

Royal Portrait

MATERIALS:

- 1 sheet of 12" x 18" construction paper
- pencil and eraser
- thin black marker
- crayons
- various examples of royal portraits (for example, *The Old King* by Georges Rouault, a king and queen from a deck of cards)

DIRECTIONS:

1. What do you notice about the way kings and queens are portrayed? Do these portraits seem serious or silly? Do the people seem stiff or relaxed? How do you know whether the person in the picture is a king or queen?

2. Answering the questions in step 1 will help you with your own Royal Portraits. Begin by creating the face for your king or queen with pencil on construction paper. Add the features of the face carefully. Try to make an expression that is similar to the ones you have observed.

3. After completing the face, you may add the hair and crown. Try to show as much detail as possible. For example, perhaps you could add the king/queen's jewels in your crown or a beard and mustache for the king.

4. To complete your portrait, you may wish to show his or her collar. Is it velvet? fur? satin?

5. When you are happy with your drawing, go over your pencil lines with a thin, black marker. Then begin to color your king or queen with crayons. Remember some colors can look more "royal" than others. Which ones? Why?

Motivational Drawings

Motivational Drawings

MATERIALS:

- **12" x 18" white drawing paper**
- **thin black marker**

DIRECTIONS:

1. Far away in outer space there exists the planet ROM. On this magnificent planet live the Roms and their cousins the Nats, who are evil and look very different from the Roms.

2. Now I have never seen a Rom, nor have I been to ROM, but I've heard that both of these creatures are something to behold.

3. They move and communicate by the most amazing means, and they can change their forms whenever they wish.

4. Most of them are large; some are tall.

5. You have been assigned to travel to this planet and draw pictures of the creatures, because they are allergic to cameras and get very sick if one is pointed at them.

6. Draw your idea of a Rom and your idea of a Nat.

Hide and Seek

Hide and Seek

MATERIALS:

- **white drawing paper**
- **pencils and erasers**
- **thin black markers**
- **crayons**

DIRECTIONS:

1. Have you ever played Hide and Go Seek? Well, prented you're "it." You are counting to 100; you have your hands over your eyes, and you are lying in a field of tall grass. Now, when you get to 50, you might start to peek through your fingers a little, and as you do, you notice the world of "tiny" things right under your nose. In this "tiny" world, the grass seems very tall compared to the size of an ant or a ladybug. Why, to an ant, one blade of grass might seem like Mt. Everest! In your pictures, try to capture as many different "creatures" as possible. Just make sure that none of them are too large. Some of the things you might include are pebbles, mushrooms, spider webs, flowers, clover, snails, butterflies, worms, spiders, caterpillars, grasshoppers, baby turtles, frogs, ladybugs, ants, beetles, centipedes, flies, and bumblebees. It's quite a busy world, even though it's a tiny one.

2. Holding your paper horizontally, begin to draw your grass. Make lines from the bottom to the top to show individual blades of grass. Some will be straight, some will be bent, some will be short, some will be long, some will be fat, some will be skinny. Most will be skinnier on the top than at the bottom. And in order to show a lot of grass in your picture, some blades of grass will have to go behind others. When this happens, simply stop your line where it meets another blade of grass and start it again on the other side. This step takes some practice, so keep your eraser handy.

3. After you have drawn as many layers as possible, outline them carefully with a thin, black marker and make sure you stay on your pencil outlines.

4. Next, use your pencil to add insects and other tiny things. Then, outline these with a marker, too.

5. Afterward, you can begin coloring in, and you may want to make your grass different shades of green. This can look very interesting when completed.

6. Your teacher may wish to display several of your pictures together when they're done. Together they can create a giant grass jungle!

Zoo Murals

Zoo Murals

MATERIALS:

- **long piece of mural-strength paper**
- **scrap papers of all kinds, including wallpaper, glazed paper, fluorescent paper, velour paper, metallic paper, magazines**
- **scissors and glue**
- **thin colored markers**
- **12" x 18" manila paper**
- **pencil and eraser**

DIRECTIONS:

1. Draw an animal that lives at the zoo.

2. Add a protective environment to keep him away from people and people away from him, but do not use a fence or a cage. Rocks, water, and gulleys can serve this purpose.

3. Adjust the environment to your animal's needs. Does he like to climb, to swim, to run? Are there places for him to hide and have privacy when he wants it?

4. Cut your animal out of the appropriate color paper.

5. Do the same for his environment.

6. Glue the animal on his environment.

7. Glue the animal and his environment on the long pieces of mural paper.

8. Add other animals and their environments.

9. Add other items for further interest such as the following: people walking, viewing the animals, and taking pictures; sidewalks; signs; trees; bushes; ticket booths; refreshment stands; and so forth.

Scratchboards

Scratchboards

MATERIALS:

- 9" x 12" sheet of oaktag or poster board
- regular and fluorescent crayons
- black tempera and brushes
- liquid dish detergent
- sharp wooden stick
- newspaper
- manila paper

DIRECTIONS:

1. Begin by drawing random shapes on the oaktag and coloring them in by pressing very hard on the crayons.

2. When this is completed, prepare your paint by adding a few drops of liquid detergent and stirring carefully. Then place your paper on top of the newspaper and brush the black paint across it in slow, even strokes. Continue this until your paper is completely black. Then put it aside to dry.

3. While it is drying, you may wish to make a practice sketch and experiment with some of the effects you can create with different types of lines in your scratchboard. See the following examples.

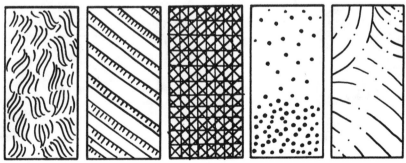

4. Once the paint has dried, you can start to "scratch" your picture into the black surface with a sharp, wooden stick. The unexpected colors will surprise you as they are revealed in your picture.

Imagination Machines

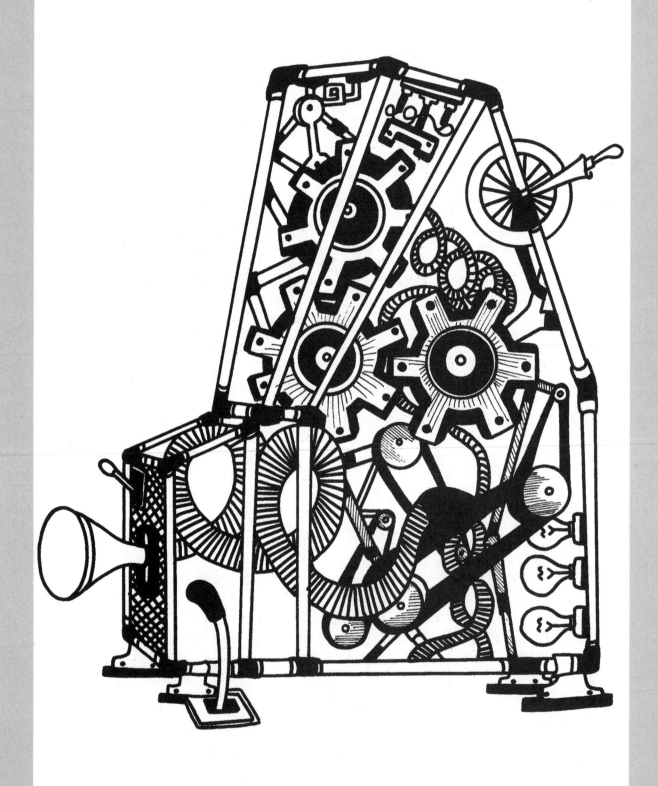

Imagination Machines

MATERIALS:

- 12" x 18" white paper
- pencil and eraser
- thin black marker
- cardboard cogs, wheels, circles, rectangles, and cylindrically shaped patterns

DIRECTIONS:

1. Think of all the machines that do jobs for us (vacuum cleaners, refrigerators, sewing machines) and that make life easier. What jobs or tasks do you do now that you would like a machine to do?

2. Look at machines in your school, that is, printers, movie projectors, and so forth.

3. Observe a collection of "machine-making stuff" including cardboard cogs and wheels in various sizes, circles, tabs, various rectangular shapes, and pipes.

4. Use black markers to draw around these shapes.

5. Add these parts together and continue with your own.

6. A "making" machine needs a place to put something in and a place for the finished product to come out, with lots of "stuff" in the middle to do the making.

7. A "doing" machine might need special switches and arms to control it and make it do its work.

8. Label your paper with the task your machine performs.

Painting

Sidewalk Paintings

LEVEL 1

Painting on a large scale, combining simple shapes, and creating a pattern through repetition are all involved in *Giant Paper Ice Cream Cones.* The next activity, *Pussy Willows,* combines drawing and painting. Students learn more about creating depth in their work when faced with the task of showing overlapping branches as they appear through a transparent surface. *Sidewalk Paintings* is an activity that encourages large, bold expression using bright colors and simple shapes.

Big Bad Bug Painting

LEVEL 2

Most paintings begin with a drawing, but in the lesson *Painted Skeletons,* students learn to build up their paintings using directly painted shapes. Fantasy and imagination are stressed in the next activity, *Big Bad Bug Painting.* Outlining with black paint, using primary colors, and reducing complex objects to simple forms are all involved in *Painted Turkeys.*

Glowing Fish

LEVEL 3

Pattern, repetition, and texture are explored using fluorescent paint on black paper to create *Glowing Fish.* In *Fabric Painting,* students are encouraged to become their own designer and create some wearable art.

Giant Paper
Ice Cream Cones

Giant Paper Ice Cream Cones

MATERIALS:

- pencil and eraser
- 12" x 18" paper
- crayons
- glue
- scissors

DIRECTIONS:

1. Think of your favorite flavor of ice cream and the fun of eating ice cream on a hot summer day.

2. Begin by drawing a triangle on the paper for the cone.

3. Cut this out.

4. Draw curved, straight, or zigzag lines across the cone and then down like a real ice cream cone design.

5. The shapes resulting from the crossed lines can be colored in brightly.

6. Think of the shape of a scoop of ice cream. Is it a plain, round ball? Imagine a big, fluffy scoop, the kind that hangs over the side of the cone. Make some curves, some bumps, some wiggles.

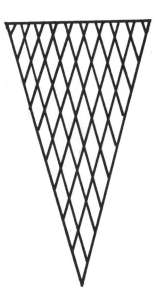

7. Cut these out. If you have trouble, cut down into the points of your ice cream scoops by first cutting down one side, then removing the scissors and cutting down the other side, rather than trying to cut down and then up.

8. Draw and cut out another smaller scoop.

9. Glue all three parts together and add a cherry on top.

10. Add treats to your scoops: cherries and berries, nuts and chocolate bits, marshmallow fluffs, strings of licorice, hearts, sprinkles.

Pussy Willows

Pussy Willows

MATERIALS:

- 12" x 18" gray paper
- thin black marker
- glass vase of pussy willows
- silver crayons
- cotton swabs
- white tempera paint

DIRECTIONS:

1. After viewing the vase of pussy willows for a few minutes, place your paper vertically in front of you.

2. Draw in the vase with your marker.

3. Next, add all of the branches using a silver crayon.

4. Make sure your willows stretch nearly to the top of your paper.

5. Dab on the pussy willow buds with a cotton swab dipped in white tempera.

Sidewalk Paintings

Sidewalk Paintings

MATERIALS:

- sidewalk or playground-surfaced area
- powdered tempera paints or large mural chalk
- plastic buckets to mix and carry paint
- large brushes
- white chalk

DIRECTIONS:

1. Using the white chalk, draw the outlines of objects you wish to paint. Make them large and simple for this larger-than-life painting.

2. Mix four or five basic colors in the buckets to a cream-soup consistency.

3. The best colors to use are white, red, orange, yellow, and green. Avoid blues, purples, and black because these colors are long lasting.

4. Begin to paint in the objects.

5. Have one bucket of clean water handy to clean brushes.

6. Do not paint over and over the same spot (built-up paint may come off on shoes).

7. If using chalk, let it soak first in water and then color in the objects as before.

8. Let dry and enjoy.

9. When you are tired of your painting, use a hose and a stiff bristle brush broom to remove. Brush stubborn spots with a little liquid soap. Paint will not harm grass.

Painted Skeletons

Painted Skeletons

MATERIALS:

- **black construction paper**
- **white tempera paint**
- **thin paintbrush**

DIRECTIONS:

1. These skeletons are quite simple to make when you think of them as a collection of simple shapes.

2. Begin at the top of your paper by outlining a half circle and then fill it in with paint. Outline a triangle but do not fill this in.

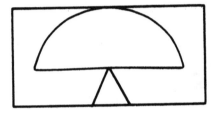

3. Next, outline two loops from the base of the triangle to each side of the half circle.

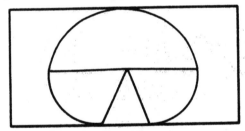

4. Then add another half circle to the base of the triangle and fill it in. Make another one (upside down) a few inches below that and also fill it in.

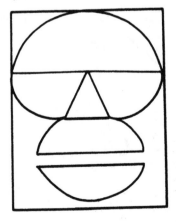 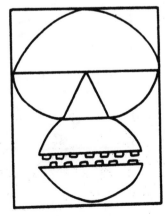

5. Next, use your brush to make small lines coming out of each half circle; these are the teeth.

6. To make your neck, add a rectangle to the bottom of your half circle with small lines sticking out of the sides.

7. Next, make the collar bone by painting a "flattened" V. Add a small circle at each end of the V. We use circles to show that two bones meet and that they can move in different directions because of "joints." Imagine how your arms would work if there were no joints! Can you feel the joint by your shoulder? Where are some other joints?

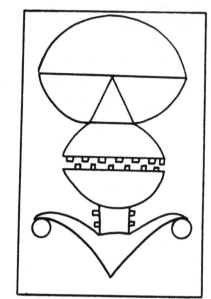

8. Paint a line to show the upper arm and then an elbow joint, then your lower arm and your wrist joint.

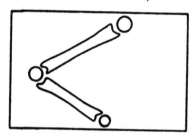

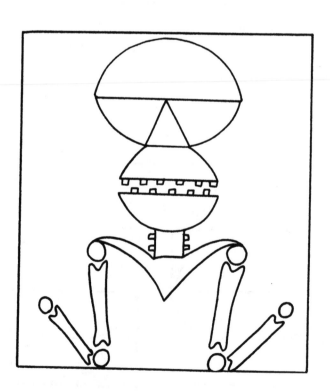

9. You can make a hand by painting a half circle and adding thin lines to show each finger. How many joints will each finger have? If you can't show all three joints, just make as many as you can.

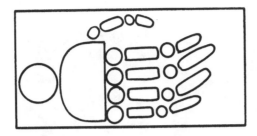

10. To create the chest, extend a line down from the center of your collar bone and show your ribs with a series of loops. Notice how the loops get smaller and smaller. Can you find your ribs? How many do you have? Try to show that many if you can.

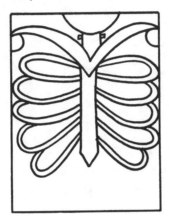

11. Next extend your body by including a line for your spine and a flattened pear shape to show your hip bone.

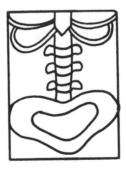

12. You can add your legs in the same way you added your arms. Remember your legs can "bend" wherever there is a "joint." Your skeleton can be shown running or jumping or just standing still.

13. Add your feet by showing the heel and the sole and the toes with all their joints.

Big Bad Bug Painting

Big Bad Bug Painting

MATERIALS:

- **tempera paints and brushes**
- **12" x 18" white drawing paper**

DIRECTIONS:

1. Think about what "bad" means to you.

2. What do you see when you hear the word "bug"—a germ or an insect?

3. How can you show that something is "big" in a painting?

4. What could a bad bug be doing? Biting someone to give the flu, sliding down someone's throat to give him or her a sore throat, fighting inside someone's body?

5. Your bug does not have to look anything like a real bug, but it might.

6. If it is an insect, it could be fighting other bugs, tearing a nest down, or biting its prey.

Painted Turkeys

Painted Turkeys

MATERIALS:

- pencil and eraser
- tempera paints and brushes
- 36" x 40" heavy yellow paper
- 9" x 12" paper

DIRECTIONS:

1. Draw a large circle on the 9" x 12" paper and a smaller circle next to it connected by two lines as shown.

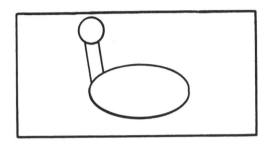

2. Add a beak, one eye, wings, a waddle, legs, and feet as shown (remember that a bird's knees bend backwards!).

3. Add overlapping ovals for feathers as shown. Three rows are usually enough.

4. Using your 9" x 12" drawing as a guide, draw the turkey again on a piece of yellow 36" x 40" paper and make your drawing large enough so that part of the turkey touches each edge of the paper. Notice how simple geometric shapes can be combined to create an object.

5. Go over all pencil lines with a brush and black tempera.

6. When dry, paint in the sections and the body with other colors, or let some sections remain the yellow color of the paper.

Glowing Fish

Glowing Fish

MATERIALS:

- **12" x 18" manila paper**
- **12" x 18" black paper**
- **fluorescent paints and brushes**
- **pencil and eraser**

DIRECTIONS:

1. Draw a basic fish shape on the manila paper. Use your own idea or one as shown.

2. Include designs to add interest to the fish, such as scallops, zigzags, stars, polka dots, and so forth.

  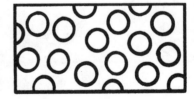

3. You might also add fancy fins or flowing tail pieces.

4. Transfer your drawing to the black paper.

5. Begin painting in the designs and the outline of the fish. Leave the inside of the body black.

Fabric Painting

Fabric Painting

MATERIALS:

- **polyester shirt**
- **fabric paint or markers**
- **9" x 12" paper**
- **black marker**
- **brushes**

DIRECTIONS:

1. Clothing has been designed and patterned in different ways for interest and decoration by people all over the world and throughout the ages.

2. Remember that a pattern is a design, line, or shape that is repeated.

3. Fold your paper in half, then in half again and again until you have eight rectangles.

4. In each rectangle, front and back, draw a different pattern so that you end up with sixteen patterns.

5. You can have lines that zigzag or scallop and shapes of different sizes, or combinations of these.

6. Notice how your shirt is made up of a variety of pieces: the cuffs, the sleeves, the yoke, the collar, two front pieces, and the back. You probably have at least nine different pieces that have been sewn together to make your shirt.

7. Using the fabric paint or markers, copy one pattern from your paper onto one piece or section of your shirt.

8. Repeat the pattern carefully for the full length of the shirt.

9. Try changing the colors of paint or markers for variety.

10. Continue until all the shirt pieces are completed with different patterns from your practice paper.

11. Let dry and wear proudly.

Color and Design

LEVEL 1

Letter Pictures is an activity that asks students to consider the letter as an element of design and to combine these new designs to create a picture. *Horizontal and Vertical Designs* is an activity that demonstrates the design possibilities in even the simplest combination of lines. Reinforcing the concept of how parts make a whole is given prominence in *Crayon Picture Puzzles.* Nature as an art form is considered in *Photograms,* which also encourages students to organize the elements of their composition. *All-Over Patterns* deals with repetition as the necessary ingredient in creating patterns.

LEVEL 2

One Shape Only clearly defines the use of geometric shapes in creating pictures. In this lesson, students learn about diversity (using one shape to compose each element in their picture) and also about repetition (repeating the same shape to create a new shape). Overlapping to create the illusion of depth, repetition of line patterns to create an explosive effect, and learning to contrast colors to give a design more impact are all involved in the lesson *Crayon Fireworks.*

LEVEL 3

In the lesson *Pattern Birds,* students are encouraged to explore different ways to represent texture through the use of design. In *Line Art,* the character and quality of different types of lines are examined.

Word Pictures are just what they sound like, pictures composed entire of words. *Sunglasses* is a lesson that incorporates fantasy with simple product design. By reducing a face to simple shapes and using a variety of different materials to create those shapes, students will be creating *Collage Portraits.* In *Costume Collage* students design their work by carefully selecting and combining different types of materials and patterns.

Photograms

Crayon Fireworks

Costume Collage

Letter Pictures

Letter Pictures

MATERIALS:

- **magazines (especially weekly news magazines with big advertising letters)**
- **scissors**
- **glue**
- **9" x 12" paper**
- **crayons**

DIRECTIONS:

1. Cut out various large letters from magazine ads.

2. Lay a few at a time on your paper and imagine how each could be part of an animal or a person: maybe a body, ears, a trunk, or a tail.

3. Lay the letters on their sides, or upside down, or backward until they remind you of part of something.

4. The letters that most resemble a face are "C," "D," "O," and "U."

5. It is a good idea to use the largest letters for the body and smaller letters for details.

6. The letters are not important as long as they are arranged in the shape of a body.

7. Use your crayons to add details and fill in the background.

8. Details are important; they help to identify the subject.

9. Remember that there should be a foreground and background to your picture.

10. Too many small objects on the paper distract from the center of interest. Develop one large image and add to it with your crayons.

11. Do not glue until finished.

Horizontal and Vertical Designs

Horizontal and Vertical Designs

MATERIALS:

- **1 sheet of white or black 12" x 18" construction paper**
- **thin strips of construction paper in various colors**
- **paste or white glue**
- **scissors**

DIRECTIONS:

1. Horizontal lines are ones that go across and vertical lines go up and down. Look around your classroom and see how many you can find. Can a person be a horizontal or vertical line? When?

2. Cut strips of construction paper in all different colors. Make some of your strips wide and some thin, some long and some short.

3. Now begin to place these strips on top of either a white or black sheet of construction paper. Arrange all the strips so that they are either horizontal or vertical lines.

4. Experiment with your strips and try to create interesting shapes with them. When you are happy with your arrangement, carefully paste or glue all your strips in place.

Crayon Picture
Puzzles

Crayon Picture Puzzles

MATERIALS:

- **9" x 12" sheet of thin shirt cardboard**
- **colored markers or crayons**
- **pencil and eraser**
- **sharp scissors**

DIRECTIONS:

1. Discuss what makes some ideas for pictures best for puzzles: some big shapes, definite lines (easier to match), variety in sizes of shapes and in colors.

2. Draw a picture on the cardboard and color it in using the markers.

3. Cut your picture up into irregular puzzle pieces.

4. Include some difficult pieces such as the ones shown.

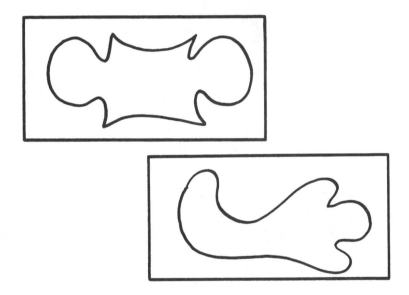

5. Some rounded bumps and uneven places help make the puzzle more fun. Sharp, thin points should be avoided because they are easily broken.

Photograms

Photograms

MATERIALS:

- **blueprint paper**
- **small, fairly flat objects from nature: grasses, leaves, flowers, weeds, feathers, and so forth**
- **shallow pan of water**
- **12" x 18" blue construction paper folded in half like a book**
- **a magazine**

DIRECTIONS:

1. For practice, arrange the objects into a design on the cover of the folded construction paper "book." Now lay objects on the blueprint paper in a fairly dark room and place inside a magazine. Close the magazine.

2. Carry the magazine, keeping it flat, outside on a sunny day.

3. Carefully open the magazine, on the ground, to your blueprint paper and the sun will begin to change the color of the paper, while the paper under the objects will remain light.

4. You may want to try moving the objects slightly to one side or another as the fading takes place for a transparent effect.

5. Depending on the kind of blueprint paper you use, you can prevent your designs from fading away. Some paper may simply be wet with water and others may be fixed in a "photographic stop fix bath."

All-Over Patterns

MATERIALS:

- **tempera paints and brushes**
- **18" x 24" construction paper**

DIRECTIONS:

1. Think of what it means to repeat something: to make the same thing over and over.

2. Think of what a pattern is: a repetition of a shape, a line, a design, or a color.

3. Think of how repetition and pattern occur in nature: bark, flowers, rainbows, fish, birds, insects, snowflakes, the insides of fruits and vegetables.

4. Think of how they are used by people: in fabric, wallpaper, clothes, rugs, jewelry.

5. Fold your piece of construction paper in half, then in half again. Continue first in one direction, then in another to form a grid or network of polygonal units.

6. Enter a single line or shape in one unit and repeat it in all the others.

7. Paint a new design element in the first unit: another line? another shape? an area colored in?

8. Repeat this element again in all the others.

9. Continue building up the design in this way—with lines, shapes, colors, accents, details—until you have an all-over pattern.

10. Mount or frame the finished pattern with another colored piece of construction paper.

One Shape Only

One Shape Only

MATERIALS:

- **12" x 18" colored construction paper**
- **glue**
- **scissors**
- **pencil and eraser**
- **construction paper scraps**

DIRECTIONS:

1. Pick one basic geometric shape: circle, rectangle, triangle, or diamond.

2. Cut various sizes and types of your shape in order to assemble objects to make a picture.

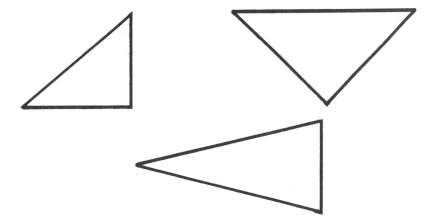

3. Once a shape has been chosen, all objects in the picture must be made from that shape; no other shape can be introduced.

Crayon Fireworks

Crayon Fireworks

MATERIALS:

- crayons   - manila paper

DIRECTIONS:

1. Begin by making a dot anywhere on your paper.

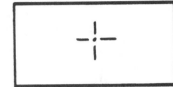

2. From your dot, draw four short lines. Put one line at the top, one at the bottom, and one line on each side. All your lines should be the same color and the same length.

3. Now add four more lines, one inside each space created by your first four lines.

4. If there is any space left between these lines, add a few more.

5. You have just completed one "explosion" of your crayon fireworks. To make it stand out, keep adding more exploding rings around the first one, but use a new color each time you start a new ring.

6. Build up each ring the same way you did for your first one.

7. When you have completed one of the fireworks, then you can add another by placing a dot somewhere else on your paper. As your paper fills up, you'll notice that some of the fireworks will have to overlap. This overlapping makes your fireworks look very exciting, as if one were bursting right after the other.

Pattern Birds

Pattern Birds

MATERIALS:

- **9" x 12" paper**
- **12" x 18" black paper**
- **thin black markers**
- **oil pastels**
- **pencil and eraser**

DIRECTIONS:

1. What is a pattern? Look at the designs in the clothes you are wearing. The shapes are repeated—this is a pattern. Patterns add interest to objects in our lives—clothing, draperies, furniture, and so forth.

2. Fold a 9" x 12" piece of paper into eight rectangles.

3. Using a thin, black marker, draw a different repeated shape or design in each to make a different pattern in each.

4. Using a pencil, draw an imaginary bird vertically on a 12" x 18" black piece of paper. As long as it has a beak, a tail, wings, and "bird" feet, it will look like a bird. What different shapes can a beak be? What about the body of a bird?

5. Birds' legs are different from ours. Our knees bend forward—birds' knees bend backward. They also have four toes—three come forward and one short toe is backward to help the birds balance.

6. Divide the bird into eight sections.

7. Draw a different pattern in each section.

8. Trace over the patterns and the outline of the bird with oil pastels.

9. You may want to color in certain areas completely.

Line Art

Line Art

MATERIALS:

- **markers**
- **oil crayons**
- **9" x 12" brightly colored paper**

DIRECTIONS:

1. Look for lines in your environment—branches, railroad tracks, roads, telephone wires, veins in a leaf, lines in a person's face, and so forth.

2. There are many kinds of lines: straight, curved, jagged, coiled, broken, heavy, delicate, and so forth.

3. Lines in a painting or a drawing serve a variety of purposes: to define shapes, to link two points, to create a path of motion in a painting, to decorate, and to create a mood.

4. In an artwork, a line can be represented by materials such as wire in a sculpture or yarn in a weaving.

5. Draw on a piece of scratch paper the following lines: a spiral line, a curved line, a snowflake line, a triangle line, and the most beautiful line in the world.

6. Select your favorite lines and, using a marker, draw them horizontally across the colored paper.

7. Look at your lines and fill in any spaces with additional designs to enhance the composition.

8. Limit the number of oil crayons you use to complete the design by adding color to the spaces and shapes formed by the lines.

Word Pictures

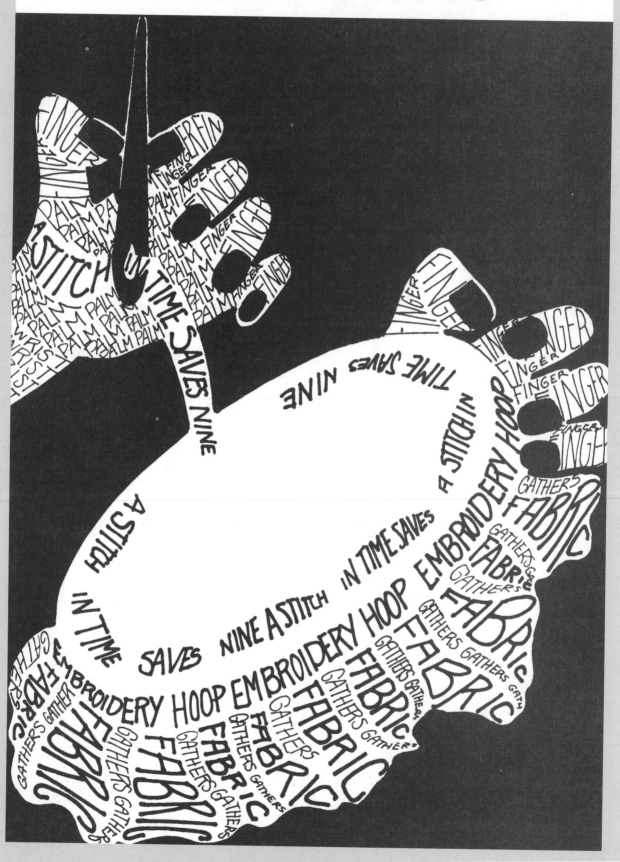

Word Pictures

MATERIALS:

- 9" x 12" white paper
- pencil, eraser, ruler
- thick black markers and thin black markers
- crayons or colored markers

DIRECTIONS:

1. Begin by selecting your subject matter. Ideas should not be very small or very detailed, or else they will be too difficult to fill in.

2. Once you've decided on your idea and sketched it onto white paper, you will then be ready to design your picture by selecting the words and the layout of the lettering.

3. You have many choices: You may wish to use words that identify each object or words that say something about it. See the following examples:

Don't outline your shapes with a marker. Outlines are created when a shape is filled in.

4. Within each shape there are many different directions your lettering can take.

5. Some lettering may be done with thick markers and some may be done with thin ones. Some lettering might look best large, while other lettering might look best small.

Sunglasses

Sunglasses

MATERIALS:

- **12" x 18" oaktag**
- **pencil and eraser**
- **scissors**
- **thin colored markers**

DIRECTIONS:

1. Draw a pair of sunglasses so that the ends reach about 2" from each end of the paper horizontally as shown.

2. Draw the lenses larger than normal.

3. Cut out the glasses but leave the lenses intact.

4. In each lens, draw a scene you would like to see if you could see only one scene through your glasses, such as an underwater scene, outer space, life on a cloud, and so forth.

5. Draw a symbol for your scene—for example, a cloud, a balloon, or a heart—and repeat it all along the frame.

6. Color in your work with the markers.

Collage Portraits

Collage Portraits

MATERIALS:

- scissors
- glue
- scrap materials for collage (fabrics, yarn, leather, straw, fake fur, buttons, construction paper, wallpaper, and so forth)
- 12" x 18" piece of chipboard or oaktag

DIRECTIONS:

1. Ask someone to model for you and observe the human head.

2. Use a ruler to check that the eyes are near the middle of the head.

3. Notice where the nose starts and ends in relation to the eyes and how close it comes to the mouth.

4. Notice the distance between the mouth and the bottom of the chin and the space between the eyes.

5. Using the collage materials, begin to cut out a large head for a portrait. Do no drawing first.

6. Cut out a neck.

7. Use other materials to add shoulders, hair, features, hats, whatever you like.

8. Make your collage portrait interesting by using a variety of materials, but select each one carefully.

9. Think of an expression for your portrait. What mood is your person in?

Costume Collage

Costume Collage

MATERIALS:

- sharp scissors and fabric or craft glue
- fabric of all kinds
- notions of all kinds: rickrack, ribbon, lace, and so forth
- raffia
- yarn
- burlap
- felt
- cotton
- crayons
- pencil and eraser

DIRECTIONS:

1. Think of a costume you would like to wear for Halloween.

2. Draw a simple outline of your head and body as shown. You may put yourself in an action position that your Halloween character might take.

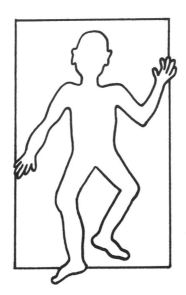

3. Cut pieces of cloth that show what your character wears and glue it to the body.

4. Glue on additional materials to help show your character more clearly.

5. Using crayons, draw in a face or add whatever else you may want in the picture.

Ceramics

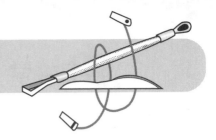

LEVEL 1

Simple clay construction techniques are introduced in the lesson *Clay Candlesticks.* Working with a ball of clay, students learn to hollow out, shape, and decorate their candlesticks. In *Ceramic Coil Mirrors,* the coil method of construction is introduced along with the technique of welding. *Clay Face Necklaces* is a lesson in pushing, pulling, pinching, and rolling clay in order to shape a desired surface. *Heart Frames and Necklaces* are created by using the slab technique along with cookie cutters. The cookie cutter not only creates the inner frame shape but also provides the shape for the necklace.

Heart Frames and Necklaces

LEVEL 2

In the lesson *Clay Bells,* students begin by creating a pinch pot and then converting it to a bell. *Clay Pockets* is an introduction to simple slab construction as well as an opportunity for students to create interesting textures and patterns in clay using a variety of tools.

Clay Pockets

LEVEL 3

Coil Pottery is a lesson that reinforces coil construction techniques while introducing their use in a three-dimensional object. In *Clay Appliqué,* students join pieces of clay to create a relief. *Evergreen Plaques* is a lesson that makes use of natural forms to create incised designs.

Coil Pottery

Clay Candlesticks

Clay Candlesticks

MATERIALS:

- **clay**
- **newspaper**
- **pencil or carving tool**
- **paint and brushes**

DIRECTIONS:

1. Take a handful of clay and roll it into a ball. (It should be about the size of a snowball.)

2. Next, place it on top of a sheet of newspaper and push it down a little in order to flatten out the bottom.

3. Now use your thumb (or a candle) to press a hole into the center of the ball.

4. Using a pencil or clay carving tool, decorate the outside with lines. You may wish to draw a picture or else just make designs.

5. After the clay has been dried thoroughly, it can be fired and then additional decoration can be done with paint.

Ceramic Coil Mirrors

Ceramic Coil Mirrors

MATERIALS:

- 3" square mirror
- clay—very moist
- mat
- heavy paper pie plate
- 2 ¾" square pieces of paper
- pencil and eraser
- clay tools
- cord

DIRECTIONS:

1. Practice rolling coils on your mat by first squeezing some clay in your hand into an elongated shape and then, using the palm of your hand, roll the coils out on your mat with slight pressure in a back and forth motion.

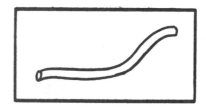

2. Trace around your square piece of paper on the inside bottom of the plate. This area will not be covered because the mirror will fit in here after the firings.

3. The side showing will be the back, and all coils have to be carefully smoothed together. Create different designs by spiraling or using different sizes of coils.

4. Dig two small holes through the frame with a clay tool. Later a cord will be strung through the holes for a hanger.

5. The plates will retain the shape of the coil frame as the clay dries.

6. Bisque, glaze, and fire again.

7. Glue the mirror to the back of the frame and string the cord through the holes.

Clay Face Necklaces

Clay Face Necklaces

MATERIALS:

- **clay**
- **pencil or clay tool**
- **newspaper**
- **paint and brushes**
- **ribbon, string, or leather strip**

DIRECTIONS:

1. Take a handful of clay and roll it into a ball; then flatten it out on a piece of newspaper until it looks like a circle.

2. Next use your pencil or clay tool to trim the edges of your circle.

3. You can begin to form your facial features by pushing or pulling the clay to raise a nose or a forehead, or a chin and cheeks.

4. You can experiment with a pencil and "draw" directly on the clay to make outlines, or you may take extra clay and roll "snakes" to make hair or balls to make pop-out eyes.

5. Use your pencil to make a hole near the top of your clay head. You should do this because when the face is completed, a string or ribbon can be threaded through the hole so that you can wear your creation.

6. When you are done shaping your face, it should be thoroughly dried and then fired. After this process you can paint your face.

Heart Frames
and Necklaces

Heart Frames and Necklaces

MATERIALS:

- clay
- rolling pin or wood cylinder
- newspaper
- silk cord or ribbon
- clay tool or dull pencil

- square cardboard pattern
- heart-shaped cookie cutter or cardboard heart pattern
- tempera paint and brushes or colored markers

DIRECTIONS:

1. On top of a sheet of newspaper, begin by rolling your clay into a ball shape and then flattening it out with both hands.

2. Next, use a rolling pin or wood cylinder to flatten the clay out very evenly.

3. Place a square cardboard pattern on top of your clay and trace around it using a clay tool or dull pencil. Remove the excess clay from the edges.

4. Next, center your heart cookie cutter in the middle of your clay square and press just lightly enough to get an outline. You don't want to cut out the shape yet. If you are using a cardboard heart pattern, the same applies. Trace around it lightly.

5. Now you are ready to decorate your frame by drawing with a tool or pencil in the areas surrounding the heart. You can make patterns or designs or even draw a scene.

6. Now you are ready to use the cookie cutter to remove the heart. After doing so, you can decorate your heart and poke a hole through it in order to be able to use it as a necklace later.

7. Both your frame and heart should be set aside to dry and then be fired.

8. After firing, hearts can be decorated with tempera paint or colored markers.

Clay Bells

Clay Bells

MATERIALS:

- clay
- modeling tools, random objects to create marks in clay
- pencil
- newspaper
- pipe cleaner
- string

DIRECTIONS:

1. On top of a sheet of newspaper, roll one handful of clay into a ball the size of a snowball.

2. Now hold the ball in your left hand while you push your right thumb directly through the center of the clay ball. Be careful not to poke your thumb right through and out the other side.

3. Now start to push your thumb against the outer walls of the clay ball while pushing and flattening the outer clay wall with your remaining fingers. This will cause the original hole that your thumb made to grow larger and larger. Continue this process until you begin to have a bowl or cup shape.

 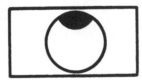  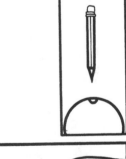

4. Next, turn your bowl upside down and carefully poke a hole through the center of the top with a pencil.

5. Roll a small clay snake and attach it above the hole. Then use a pencil or clay tool to create a face on the front of your bell; you can add hats, hair, ears, and so forth.

6. Make a small clay ball and poke a hole with a pencil right through the middle of it.

7. Set aside your clay pieces until they are thoroughly dry; then fire them. Fire the clay high so the sound of the bell will be good.

8. Assemble your bell by tying a knot in a length of string and "threading" it through the hole in the top of your bell and tie it to the handle.

Clay Pockets

Clay Pockets

MATERIALS:

- **red clay for kiln firing or self-hardening clay**
- **oval cardboard shape**
- **two 10" strips of lattice**
- **rolling pin**
- **clay modeling tools**
- **assorted textural objects (shells, tools for leather tooling, combs, gears, and so forth)**
- **mat**
- **cloth**
- **clear glaze**

DIRECTIONS:

1. Roll out a ball of clay between two lattice strips to ensure a uniformly thick slab.

2. Lay the oval cardboard shape on the slab and, using a thin modeling tool, cut around the cardboard as if you were cutting out a giant cookie.

3. Set aside the extra clay.

4. Place the oval vertically in front of you and "twirl" the end of a modeling tool through the clay about ½" from the top, which will enable it to be hung.

5. Gently fold the bottom part of the oval over one hand, which you should lay on the clay to form a pocket as shown. You might also stuff the cavity with newspaper, which will burn up in the firing process.

6. Using your thumb, gently press together where the edges of the clay now touch, leaving the pocket open as shown.

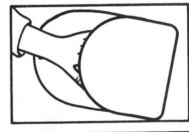

7. Leave your thumb prints as a textural interest and add more texture by using various objects previously mentioned.

8. Let the clay dry slowly by keeping it covered with a slightly damp cloth.

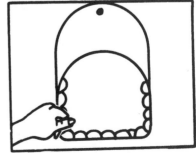

9. Fire and glaze or leave unglazed.

10. Dried flowers or grasses may be placed in the pocket.

Coil Pottery

Coil Pottery

MATERIALS:

- clay for kiln or self-hardening clay
- plastic bowls
- thin plastic bags and ties
- mats

DIRECTIONS:

1. Open a plastic bag and place it inside the plastic bowl. Make the bag conform to the shape of the inside of the bowl. Let the remainder of the plastic bag overlap its sides.

2. Take a small ball of clay and squeeze it slightly into an elongated shape like a hot dog.

3. Lay the clay on a mat and gently roll it into a coil or a "snake" using the fingers of both hands and pressing slightly as you roll together.

4. Wind this coil up to make a base for your post as shown.

5. Smooth the top only with your fingers so that you cannot see the coils on this one side.

6. Place this coil base in the bottom of your bowl on the plastic and add whatever coils are needed to completely cover the bottom.

7. Roll shorter coils and wind them as you did with the base. Begin using these to cover the inside of the bow, starting around the base and continuing upward as shown.

8. Continue to add more small, wound coils all the way around and above the previous rows, against the inside of the bowl until you reach the rim.

9. Gently smooth the entire inside of the bowl with your fingers.

10. Do not press too hard or you will also smooth out the coil design on the side facing the bowl.

11. Work that is stopped in progress can be preserved by gently closing the bag and sealing it with a twist tie so that no more air enters the bag.

12. When finished, leave the bag open but loosely pushed into the bowl so that it can dry slowly.

13. When thoroughly dry, remove the bag by gently pulling up on the bag and down on the plastic bowl. Then gently pull off the plastic bag.

14. Your bowl should then be allowed to dry further until it no longer feels cool against your cheek.

15. The bowl can be glazed after one firing and then fired once more.

Clay Appliqué Plaque

Clay Appliqué Plaque

MATERIALS:

- clay for kiln firing or self-hardening clay
- two 10" lattice strips
- rolling pin
- 2 mats
- modeling tools
- oaktag
- ribbon or yarn

DIRECTIONS:

1. Draw a circle or oval on oaktag that is precisely the size of the plaque you want and cut it out.

2. Roll the clay between two lattice strips with a rolling pin to achieve a slab of uniform thickness and place it on one of the mats.

3. Lay the pattern on the slab and cut around it with a thin modeling tool, as though you were cutting out a giant cookie.

4. Carefully remove any excess slab pieces and set them aside on the other mat.

5. About ½" from the top of the plaque, twirl a tool through the clay to make a hole for hanging.

6. Using a thin modeling tool, cut desired appliqués (shapes) out of the extra slab pieces to make a picture and lay them on the plaque.

7. Using a modeling tool, gently push clay from the edges of the applied pieces downward in order to attach them to the plaque. Marks can then be smoothed out with your index finger or left as a part of the decoration.

8. Part of the picture could be drawn with incised lines using the modeling tools.

9. Let the clay dry slowly under a damp cloth so that it will not buckle.

10. Fire and glaze your plaque and shellac it.

11. A piece of yarn or ribbon can be placed through the hole to hang it.

Evergreen Plaques

Evergreen Plaques

MATERIALS:

- oval cardboard shape
- clay for kiln firing or self-hardening clay
- two 10" lattice strips
- rolling pin
- clay modeling tools
- piece of evergreen
- mat
- glaze or tempera and shellac
- cloth
- green printing ink

DIRECTIONS:

1. Roll out a ball of clay between two lattice strips to ensure a uniformly thick slab.

2. Lay the oval cardboard shape on the slab and, using a thin modeling tool, cut around the cardboard as if you were cutting out a giant cookie.

3. Set aside the extra clay.

4. Place a piece of evergreen on the clay and lightly roll the rolling pin over it until an impression has been made in the clay.

5. Gently pull out the evergreen piece and let the clay dry slowly with a damp cloth over it.

6. When dry, fire the plaque and glaze or paint it as desired.

7. An alternate method for finishing is to wipe green printing ink over the plaque after firing, and then to keep wiping it with a damp cloth until the pine impression has absorbed most of the ink and the remainder of the surface is a light tint.

8. Let dry and shellac.

Paper Crafts

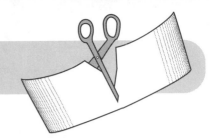

LEVEL 1

In the first activity, *Torn Paper Trees,* small torn paper shapes are arranged to create a mosaic-like tree with brightly colored leaves. *Paper Bag Houses* are three-dimensional constructions that employ a variety of simple paper sculpture techniques. The lesson *Stitched Paper Puppets* introduces puppetry, as well as simple sewing, as a technique for joining pieces of paper. The craft of paper quilling is introduced and explored in the next activity, *Quilling Valentines.*

Stitched Paper Puppets

LEVEL 2

Paper Sculpture Animals are created by using a wide variety of paper sculpture techniques. Students are encouraged to bend, fold, roll, crumple, crimp, curl, or pleat in order to create their animals. In the next lesson, paper *Witches* come alive when their paper parts are assembled and then joined with brass fasteners. In *Oaktag Houses,* basic architectural concepts are introduced and then put into practice as students create a three-dimensional building using stiff paper. Kite making is introduced and the unique qualities of tissue paper explored in the lesson *Tissue Paper Fish Kites. Two-Cardboard Relief* is an introduction to relief that uses cardboard layers to build up the varying surface levels in the composition. *Dancing Bears* are simple, fun paper toys that come to life when students learn to "let their fingers do the walking" for these ballroom bears.

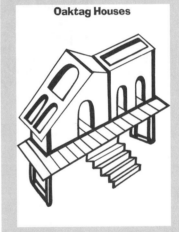

Oaktag Houses

LEVEL 3

Landscape in the Round explores the spatial relationships that exist between the different elements in a landscape. *Lunar Shadow Box* stresses imagination and inventiveness as students create a unique environment using primarily found objects and scrap materials. *Paper Bag People* are characters created by stuffing, shaping, stapling, and painting various paper bags. The silhouette is introduced and used as an overlay on a tissue paper collage background in *Tissue Paper Silhouettes.*

Tissue Paper Silhouettes

Torn Paper Trees

Torn Paper Trees

MATERIALS:

- **12" x 18" blue paper**
- **glue or paste**
- **scraps of paper: brown, orange, yellow, green**

DIRECTIONS:

1. Imagine how a tree grows: The roots take hold in the ground, the trunk thickens, and branches divide from it; they then divide again and get thinner until they are the tiny twigs on the ends of the branches. Leaves come out and then begin to fall in the autumn.

2. Tear out a big, wide trunk for your "tree" from the brown scrap paper.

3. You will have an easier time if you tear the paper slowly with little movements of your fingers.

4. Glue the trunk on your blue paper.

5. Tear out a few big branches to extend off the trunk and glue these on your paper.

6. Tear out thinner, shorter branches or twigs and glue these so that they extend off the few big branches.

7. Tear some leaves out of the remaining colors and glue some of them on the branches and some on the ground to show ones that have fallen.

Paper Bag Houses

Paper Bag Houses

MATERIALS:

- **lunch bag**
- **assorted colored paper**
- **markers or paint and brushes**
- **cardboard**
- **white glue**
- **crumpled newspaper**
- **stapler**

DIRECTIONS:

1. Lay a lunch bag in front of you, still flat, with the top of the bag pointing away from you.

2. Add features such as doors, windows, shutters, and chimneys by using white glue and pieces of colored paper.

3. Open up the bag and stuff it with two single sheets of crumpled newspaper.

4. Fold the top over once or twice and staple, taking care to make sure the bag retains a box-like shape.

5. Fold one sheet of construction paper in half and staple over the top of the bag to create the roof.

6. Cardboard may be glued to the base of the house to allow room for trees, fences, mailboxes, people, and cars.

7. Additional details can be added with markers or paint.

Stitched Paper Puppets

Stitched Paper Puppets

MATERIALS:

- **2 pieces of brown 12" x 18" butcher paper**
- **tempera paints and brushes**
- **yarn and yarn needles**
- **pencil and eraser**
- **scissors**

DIRECTIONS:

1. Lay your hand and part of your arm on one piece of paper.

2. Around this draw a large character for your puppet. Draw it as large as possible on the paper.

3. Possible characters might be a clown, baseball player, a princess, and so forth.

4. Remove your arm and add features and details.

5. Cut out and place on a second piece of paper.

6. Trace around except for the feet.

7. Paint with bold, bright colors.

8. Let dry.

9. Stitch using an overlapping stitch front to back with yarn. Leave a large opening at the puppet's feet.

Quilling Valentines

Quilling Valentines

MATERIALS:

- **3 doilies**
- **2 sheets of red 9" x 12" construction paper**
- **thin strips of white paper**
- **white glue**
- **scissors and pencil**

DIRECTIONS:

1. Arrange three medium-sized doilies on a sheet of 9" x 12" red construction paper so that they overlap like this. Then glue them in place.

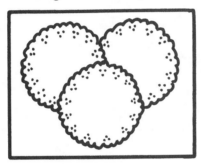

2. Next, fold your other 9" x 12" sheet of red construction paper in half and draw half of a heart starting at the fold as shown.

3. Cut it out, center it on top of your doilies and then glue it in place.

4. Next, take a thin, strip of white paper and roll it around a pencil or crayon. Then slide it off the pencil (but don't let it uncurl yet) and dip it into a puddle of white glue. (Your "puddle" should be in a plastic lid or on top of scrap cardboard.) Next, place it along the outline of your heart and let it uncurl a little as you hold it in place to dry.

5. Continue to make and add spirals until your heart is full.

Paper Sculpture Animals

Paper Sculpture Animals

MATERIALS:

- **9" x 12" white and colored construction paper**
- **stapler and masking tape**
- **scissors**
- **glue**

A **mural** is a large artwork hung or made directly on a wall. A mural can be made of a variety of materials such as paint, chalk, paper, wood, and so forth. Usually a theme is chosen, such as a zoo, a circus, the classroom, a city, a farm, a jungle, an undersea world. This offers the opportunity to explore composition on a larger scale. In museums you can see examples of Greek, Egyptian, and Chinese murals. Early people drew murals of animals and hunting scenes on the walls of their caves.

DIRECTIONS:

1. Think of your favorite zoo animal: an elephant, a giraffe, a bear, a monkey, and so on.

2. Think about the appearance of each animal: the long legs and long neck of the giraffe, a squirrel's bushy tail, a camel's hump, an elephant's long trunk, and a kangaroo's strong hind legs.

3. Flat paper has two directions or dimensions: width and length. A three-dimensional object has another direction: depth or thickness.

4. You can make a flat piece of paper stand by itself. You can fold it, curve it, or roll it and fasten it to make a cylinder. It can also be crumpled to make it stand.

5. You can run the paper over the blade of a scissors or roll the paper around a pencil to make it curl.

6. Try cutting a line into the center of a paper and then overlapping the edges. This will mound the paper up into a cone.

7. Try folding a piece of paper these ways: into hinges, into box-like shapes, into reverse pleats, folding two strips of paper over and over each other to make a spring-like object.

8. Try crumpling a piece of paper. It can be left as a ball, or it can be opened again into an almost flat, bumpy paper.

9. Don't use any pencils or make drawings first. Don't add any details with pencil or crayon. If the parts are too small to cut from the paper, they are too small to show.

10. Decide what kind of an animal you would like to make, and then choose your paper.

11. Be sure you make the animal strong enough to stand. Make its legs the same length so that it can stand easily. Make sure your animal balances to stand alone.

12. Make several animals for your zoo.

Witches

Witches

MATERIALS

- pencil and eraser
- green, black, brown construction paper
- scissors
- glue
- 4 brass fasteners
- thin black marker

DIRECTIONS:

1. Draw and cut out the profile (side view of a person's face and nose where you see only one eye) of a witch's face on green paper. Make her have a pointed chin, a crooked nose, and a narrow, wicked eye. Be sure to include a neck.

2. Draw and cut out a crooked witch's hat and stringy hair and glue them onto the head of the witch.

3. Draw and cut out a ragged dress shape on black paper—as shown— with an opening for the neck.

4. Glue the neck underneath the dress opening.

5. To make each arm for your witch, use green paper to draw the two separate shapes, as shown, and cut them out. One shape is the upper arm and the other is the lower arm and hand.

 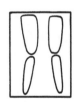 

6. Glue the top of the arm parts under the sleeve openings.

7. On green paper, draw one pair of the two leg parts, as shown, for the thigh area and the calf area.

8. Glue the tops of the leg parts under the dress opening.

9. Attach the tops and bottoms of the arms and legs together with a brass fastener, which you push through both pieces. Spread the "wings" of the fasteners to hold them in place. Overlap the leg parts slightly at the knees and the arm parts at the elbows to enable your witch to bend just as we do.

10. Cut out shoes and glue them on the legs.

11. Cut and glue an object for your witch to hold, such as a broom, a cat, a pumpkin, and so forth.

Oaktag Houses

Oaktag Houses

MATERIALS:

- oaktag
- 9" x 12" heavy cardboard
- scissors and glue
- craft sticks or tongue depressors and cotton swabs
- ruler

DIRECTIONS:

1. Ask yourself if you would rather be in a tent or a glass house, a cozy tree house or a soft, warm, sunny field.

2. These are all very different spaces, and you would feel differently living in each.

3. Look at pictures or slides of a variety of buildings and architecture. As you view the pictures, ask yourself which buildings look strong, and which look light and airy.

4. Using the oaktag, sticks, and swabs, make a shelter that has a feeling of openness.

5. To make it easier to glue corners, you should draw and cut each so that each has a fold to overlap and glue together.

6. To make folding easier, hold a ruler on the fold line and fold over, or either run or score a single blade of the scissors on the line of the fold.

7. Cut out windows and doors before gluing them on the cardboard base.

Tissue Paper Fish Kites

Tissue Paper Fish Kites

MATERIALS:

- **tissue paper and construction paper**
- **white glue**
- **pipe cleaner**
- **string**
- **thin marker**
- **scissors**

DIRECTIONS:

1. On one large, folded sheet of construction paper, draw your fish making sure that the tail touches one end of the paper and the mouth touches the other end. Keep your outline simple. Extend the length of the mouth, because this will later be folded back.

2. Cut out your fish and place it on top of two sheets of tissue paper. Trace around the fish with a marker and cut through both sheets on the outline.

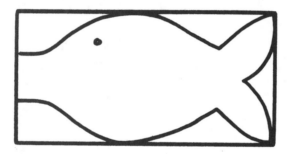

3. Use additional tissue paper to cut out fish scales. Attach these with white glue to each side of your fish and then glue the two sides together. Do not glue the tail or mouth closed so that the wind can pass through the kite when flown.

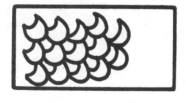 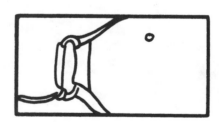

4. Fold back the mouth and slide a pipe cleaner through the fold; twist it closed and glue down the fold with white glue. Bend the pipe cleaner a bit to open the mouth; attach a piece of string.

5. Cut long, thin strips of tissue paper and attach these with white glue to the tail.

Two-Cardboard Relief

Two-Cardboard Relief

MATERIALS:

- 12" x 18" heavy cardboard
- thin shirt cardboard or the inside of a corrugated cardboard shoe box top for a simple picture that also provides a frame
- scissors and glue
- pencil and eraser
- tempera paints and brushes

Relief is a picture or design made up of surfaces that are raised from the background by the thickness of one or more layers.

DIRECTIONS:

1. Think of a scene where exciting action is taking place: a fire in a high-rise, an elephant stampede in the jungle, two dinosaurs in fierce combat, and so forth.

2. Begin to cut out the larger objects or shapes needed for your picture and glue them on the heavy cardboard.

3. Continue with medium-size shapes and then small ones.

4. Check to see that your space is filled properly and that you have fully told your exciting story by including enough objects, people, or animals.

5. Is the weather an important factor to consider in order to heighten the excitement of your picture?

6. In some places, have smaller pieces of cardboard on top of others to create more of a relief effect.

7. Paint all cardboard shapes with tempera and let dry.

Dancing Bears

Dancing Bears

MATERIALS:

- **oaktag, posterboard, or thin cardboard**
- **crayons or markers**
- **pencils and scissors**
- **glue**
- **felt**

DIRECTIONS:

1. Begin by outlining your bear on a piece of oaktag approximately 4" x 6". You can lay out your bear by using a series of circles. See the following illustration. Note that you are not drawing legs on the bear.

2. Next, outline the arms and add clothes: a bow tie and top hat or perhaps a tutu and crown. Then draw two circles in the space where the legs would begin. See the illustration on the right.

3. Now, use markers or crayons to color and decorate your bear. When this is done, cut out the bear and poke a hole into each of the leg circles and cut those out as well.

4. Insert your index and middle fingers through the holes and your bear is ready to "dance."

Landscape in the Round

Landscape in the Round

MATERIALS:

- **oaktag**
- **stapler**
- **scissors**
- **markers**
- **colored construction paper**

DIRECTIONS:

1. You are going to build a landscape—any scene outdoors—right here.

2. Four things will be needed: (1) the baseline (ground or water); (2) objects at, below, or slightly above this line; (3) objects in the sky; and (4) space.

3. Objects cannot float in space by themselves (except in outer space), away from gravity, or in water (where they need water in order to float).

4. Objects must be related to each other: boats and fish need water, houses and volcanoes need land. Clouds, the sun, planes, and parachutists somewhere must touch objects that project from a baseline in order to express their relationship to them.

5. In our real world, clouds, stars, and a rising sun at the horizon are intruded upon by hills, houses, and trees.

6. Overlapping oaktag shapes will capture this arrangement.

7. Don't arrange the landscape flat on a table because you will not be able to see the spaces between the objects. These spaces are important, so do your arranging by holding your landscape up and away from you.

8. Begin by cutting a piece of oaktag 18″ x 3″. Circle this around and staple so that it will sit on a table.

9. This will be your ground or water.

10. Build from here and/or on this piece.

11. Space is captured between objects by joining sky objects in an over-arch pattern, like an umbrella.

12. At least two sky objects must touch opposite land or sea areas for balance.

13. Did you include vehicles or people in your landscape?

Lunar Shadow Boxes

Lunar Shadow Boxes

MATERIALS:

- shoe box
- colored cellophane
- tape
- glue and scissors
- cotton
- scrap materials of all kinds: wood, fabric, notions, yarn, boxes, string, and so forth

DIRECTIONS:

1. Turn a shoe box on its side and think of the inside as the dark side of the moon—the side no one has seen. Do you think anything lives there? What kind of objects make up a "moonscape"?

2. You may want to suspend objects on strings or build objects on the bottom. What do you think the surface would be like?

3. Creatures, buildings, animals, or vehicles may be added.

4. When the inside is finished, cover the front with a light-colored cellophane that has been cut a little larger than the opening and glued to the sides.

Paper Bag People

Paper Bag People

MATERIALS:

- **paper lunch bags**
- **stapler**
- **newspaper**
- **paper and cardboard**
- **tempera and brushes**
- **starch**
- **cloth**
- **colored tissue paper**
- **black markers**
- **gloss acrylic polymer**
- **yarn**
- **glue and scissors**

DIRECTIONS:

1. Stuff the bags with crushed and torn newspaper. Whole or parts of bags can be used.

2. Staple bags together as has been done in the figure shown.

3. Staple on cardboard hands and feet as shown.

4. Glue on additional paper parts such as eyes, nose, mouth, hats, and paper curls or yarn for hair.

5. Paint with tempera mixed with starch.

6. Use cloth or colored tissue for clothing.

Tissue Paper Silhouettes

Tissue Paper Silhouettes

MATERIALS:

- assorted pastel colors of tissue paper
- tissue collage glue or watered-down white glue
- 1 sheet of 12" x 18" white paper
- 1 sheet of 9" x 12" black paper
- pencils, and scissors
- glue brushes
- manila practice paper

DIRECTIONS:

1. To begin, tear interesting shapes from different pastel-colored sheets of tissue paper.

2. Arrange these shapes on your white paper. Move the shapes around until you find a pleasing arrangement. Perhaps a collection of shapes will start to look like something you recognize: a wave, a mountain, a sunset, a forest. If it does, you may want to tear additional shapes more deliberately so that you can control the scene you are creating. You do not *have* to create a scene because in these pictures a random design will also work nicely.

3. Brush the glue over the tissue paper to keep the shapes in place. Fill up every bit of your paper. When you get to the edges of your paper, you can let the tissue overhang and trim this excess off later when it's dry.

4. After filling your entire paper with shapes, put it aside to dry.

5. While you are waiting, you can begin to sketch your silhouettes. You may wish to make some practice sketches on manila paper to see what kinds of things make good silhouettes. Remember that silhouettes rely on the details provided in their outlines to show what they are.

6. Once you've decided, draw your silhouette on black paper, cut it out, and use glue to attach it to your tissue paper background.

Printmaking

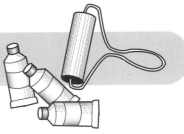

LEVEL 1

The first activity in this chapter, *Handprints,* is a lesson in the simplest form of printmaking. Students produce a print of their hand by making a direct impression of it in clay. The concept of texture, both visual and tactile, is introduced in *Texture Prints.* Printmaking from a stencil is introduced in the lesson *Chalk Prints.*

LEVEL 2

Two-Color Styrofoam Prints is an activity that introduces two-color printmaking with the use of negative and positive space. *Tempera Tile Prints* provides an introduction to the printing brayer as well as to the use of found objects in creating a pressed print. *Leaf Prints* provides further exploration of the incised print as well as an opportunity to work directly from nature.

LEVEL 3

Gadget Prints reinforces the use of found objects in printmaking as well as the process of pressed prints.

Texture Prints

Two-Color
Styrofoam Prints

Gadget Prints

Handprints

Handprints

MATERIALS:

- **clay**
- **newspaper**
- **rolling pin or wood cylinder**
- **clay tool or dull pencil**
- **cardboard circle**
- **spray paint or tempera paint and polymer**
- **brushes**
- **ribbon**

DIRECTIONS:

1. Handprints are one of the simplest forms of printmaking. Captured in clay, they will last forever.

2. Begin by rolling your clay into the shape of a large ball. Next, place it on top of some newspaper and begin to flatten out the ball by pushing down on it with both hands.

3. Next, use a rolling pin to flatten it out evenly.

4. Place a cardboard circle (large enough to fit your hand) on top of the clay and trace around it with a clay tool or dull pencil. Remove the extra clay from the edges.

5. Now you are ready to print by simply placing your right hand in the center of your clay circle and pressing down on it with your left hand to get a clear impression.

6. You may wish to write your name and date on the plaque and create designs all around the edge with a clay tool or dull pencil.

7. Using your pencil, make a hole near the top of your plaque; then set it aside to dry.

8. After firing, plaques can be spray painted or painted with tempera and then coated with polymer. A ribbon can be looped through the hole in the top of the plaque and tied in a bow if so desired.

Texture Prints

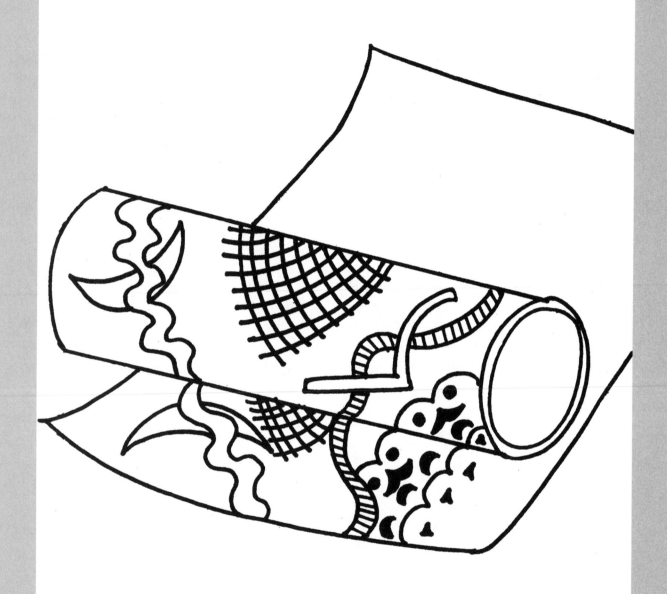

Texture Prints

MATERIALS:

- cardboard tube from toilet paper or paper towel roll
- scissors and glue
- scrap flat materials that have a texture or design: fabric, rickrack, ribbon, felt, burlap, trims, paper straws, pipe cleaners, yarn, doilies, wallpaper with raised designs, corrugated cardboard, and so forth
- water-based printing ink
- brayers
- tray or cookie sheet to roll out ink
- various printing papers

DIRECTIONS:

1. Select items that have an interesting texture.

2. Glue pieces of the items all around the cardboard tube. Be sure to glue the pieces completely flat and securely.

3. Let dry completely.

4. Roll out ink on your tray.

5. Either roll the cardboard tube on a tray or use a brayer to roll ink onto the tube until its surface is well inked. Work quickly before the ink dries.

6. Slowly roll the tube on a piece of printing paper using your fingers inside the tube to print the various designs onto the paper. A broom handle or large dowel may be placed inside the tube when rolling to provide more pressure.

7. Let dry.

Chalk Prints

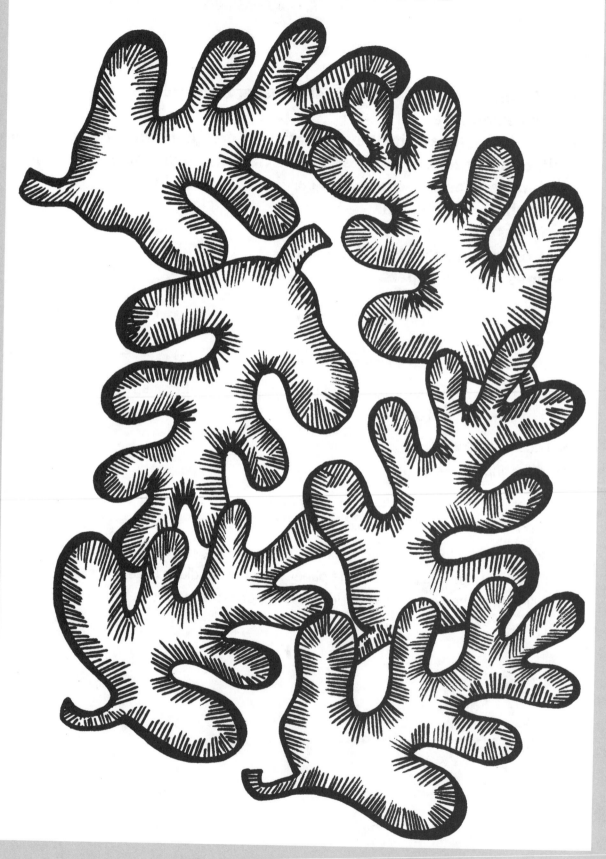

Chalk Prints

MATERIALS:

- oaktag or lightweight cardboard
- colored chalk
- tissues
- construction paper
- pencils
- scissors
- newspaper

DIRECTIONS:

1. The first thing you must do is make a stencil. To do this you must decide upon an idea for your picture because your stencil will be a shape that is repeated many times in your picture.

2. Once you've decided, draw your shape on a piece of oaktag.

3. Next, poke a hole through the middle of your shape using one blade of your scissors so that you can cut to the edges of your outline.

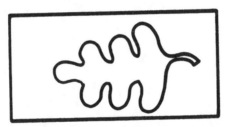

4. Next, place your stencil on top of a piece of newspaper while you color with chalk near the edges of your shape.

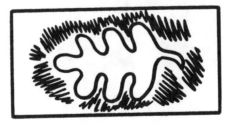

5. Now you are ready to place your stencil on top of your construction paper (with the chalked side up) and take a tissue so that you can rub the chalk off the oaktag into the cutout space, thereby making a print.

6. Repeat this process again and again to create your picture. Rechalk your stencil as necessary.

7. Notice what interesting things happen when you overlap your prints.

Two-Color Styrofoam Prints

Two-Color Styrofoam Prints

MATERIALS:

- **washed Styrofoam meat trays**
- **water-soluble printing ink in contrasting colors**
- **plastic trays for rolling ink**
- **brayers**
- **printing paper**
- **newspapers**
- **scissors**

DIRECTIONS:

1. Animals use camouflage for survival. Camouflage in natures uses color and pattern on an animal's skin, fur, or feathers to enable it to blend into its environment. By blending in, the animal cannot be seen so easily by other animals or by people.

2. Obvious examples include a leopard, snakes, a tiger, and birds.

3. Trim the edges off the tray so you can work with a flat surface.

4. Use one point of the scissors and carefully draw an environment in the soft Styrofoam.

5. Use a brayer to roll the printing ink onto the Styrofoam tray.

6. Place a piece of paper on top of the inked tray, and roll a clean brayer along the paper, or rub the paper with the pads of your fingers.

7. Carefully lift the inked tray off the paper.

8. Allow the print to dry.

9. Trim the edges off a second tray.

10. Draw the animal that lives in the already-printed environment and completely cut it out.

11. Repeat the inking procedure.

12. Place the inked animal on top of the dried environment print.

13. By gently pressing, the animal will become imprinted on the previous print.

Tempera Tile Prints

Tempera Tile Prints

MATERIALS:

- tempera
- acrylic gloss medium
- 1/16" thick pieces of poster or illustration board
- hard and soft brayers
- plastic trays to roll paint
- found objects for printing
- brush to roll tempera
- water

DIRECTIONS:

1. Roll the brayer over one tempera paint color in the plastic tray and roll in successive layers on a piece of illustration board.

2. Roll different colors, one over the other.

3. Pick found objects with which to print.

4. Paint tempera on the part of the found object that has a textured surface and print over the brayer layers previously done. One object may be used in repetition as an all-over pattern or several objects may be combined in a controlled design.

5. Let dry.

6. Paint a coat of acrylic gloss medium over the ink. Smooth out any brush strokes. You may find that you want to thin this medium with a little water.

Leaf Prints

Leaf Prints

MATERIALS:

- **assorted green leaves (leaves should be fresh and supple)**
- **9" x 12" newsprint paper**
- **scissors and glue**
- **black water-based printing ink**
- **brayer**
- **shallow pan or cookie sheet**
- **12" x 18" piece of color construction paper**
- **magazine**

DIRECTIONS:

1. Open a magazine and lay a leaf with the veined side (usually also the lighter side) up.

2. Roll ink in the pan and, holding the stem of the leaf, gently roll the ink from the stem outward at different angles.

3. Do not try to cover the entire leaf with ink. Rather, try to be able to see the network of veins as this will add an interesting pattern to your print.

4. Remove the leaf and place it ink side up on the next magazine page.

5. Lay the piece of newsprint on top of the leaf and gently rub. You will feel the veins and begin to see a faint impression of the leaf through the paper.

6. Gently peel the paper from the leaf and let the print dry.

Gadget Prints

Gadget Prints

MATERIALS:

- **kitchen or household gadgets, such as can openers, graters, forks, egg beaters, bottle stoppers, pizza cutters, potato mashers, corks, spools, clothespins, bottle tops, corkscrews, spatulas, and so forth**
- **tempera and small brushes**
- **12" x 18" colored construction paper**

DIRECTIONS:

1. Brush paint on a side of an object that has an interesting shape for a print.

2. Press the object on a piece of paper to produce a print.

3. Repeat the above with other objects and paint colors.

4. You could try making a design or a picture from the objects.

Weaving

Straight Weaving

Circle Weaving

Paper Weaving

LEVEL 1

The first activity *Straight Weaving,* introduces the concept of weaving and the basic techniques involved in this craft. New vocabulary is introduced as students learn the meaning of loom, warp, weft, and weave. The characteristics of different types of yarn are considered as students select and combine them in their work.

LEVEL 2

The next activity, *Circle Weaving,* reinforces basic weaving techniques while introducing a new type of loom. Further attention is placed on the selection and placement of different types of yarn in order to create contrast and patterns in their work.

LEVEL 3

The technique of weaving without a loom is introduced in the lesson *Paper Weaving.* In this lesson, students weave together large pieces of construction paper and the result is a large paper heart. In the lesson *Straw Weaving,* a new and unique type of loom, comprised of straws, is introduced. A weaving variation is explored in the next activity, *Ojos de Dios.* It involves the creation of designs and patterns in yarn as it is wound around wooden spokes.

Straight Weaving

Straight Weaving

MATERIALS:

- 6" x 8" piece of cardboard or Styrofoam meat tray (If Styrofoam is used, place a strip of masking tape at each short end before cutting notches.)
- scissors
- skein of yarn
- scrap yarn
- pencil and eraser
- simple ruler (inches only)
- masking tape
- stick or branch slightly wider than the cardboard

Weaving is the intertwining of materials. Materials used include yarn, cord, grasses, ribbon, and so forth. Weaving can be done to produce a useful article or an artwork. A design or pattern can be planned, or the work can be spontaneous and random. Weaving has been done for thousands of years. In museums we can see examples of Egyptian, South American, Indian, and Polynesian weavings. In colonial America, cloth was woven for clothes, draperies, and coverlets.

DIRECTIONS:

1. Using the ruler, mark one-inch notches about a half-inch in length across both of the six-inch ends of the cardboard or Styrofoam as shown.

2. Take the end of the yarn on a skein and tape it to the back of the cardboard just below one of the first notches.

3. Run this through the notch to the front side.

4. Continue the yarn strand directly across to the next notch. Go through that notch, around the back of the notch immediately next to it, and back through that notch to the front again.

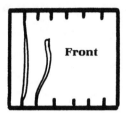

5. Continue the strand of yarn directly across to the next notch, around to the back and through the next notch all the way across the cardboard until you run out of notches. Tape the yarn strand on the back and cut.

6. Your weaving should look like this:

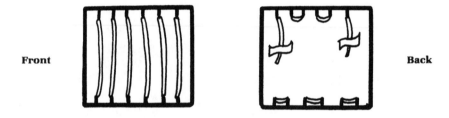

7. Cut a length of another color or type of yarn (no longer than two feet).

8. Tape one end of this yarn to the back of the cardboard as shown in "A." Bring the other end of the yarn around to the front and begin weaving over and under each yarn strand as shown in "B."

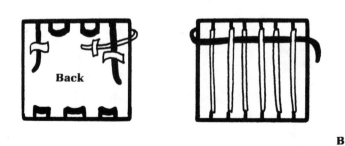

A   B

9. Take the same strand of yarn and weave back the opposite way, going over a strand you went under before and under a strand you went over before as shown below.

10. Continue weaving each new row, alternating the "over–under" pattern each time.

11. When you run out of a color, simply start with the new strand exactly where you ended the old, continuing the over–under pattern.

12. Push each row up against the next, but *do not* pull each strand tight after each line of weaving. If you do pull each strand of weaving, your weaving will look curved like this instead of straight.

13. When you can no longer weave any more strands of yarn through, undo the tape and discard it. Pull the loops of yarn gently out of their notches and tie any ends of yarn to the nearest loop.

14. Weave a stick or branch through the top loops of the weaving and hang as a wall hanging.

Circle Weaving

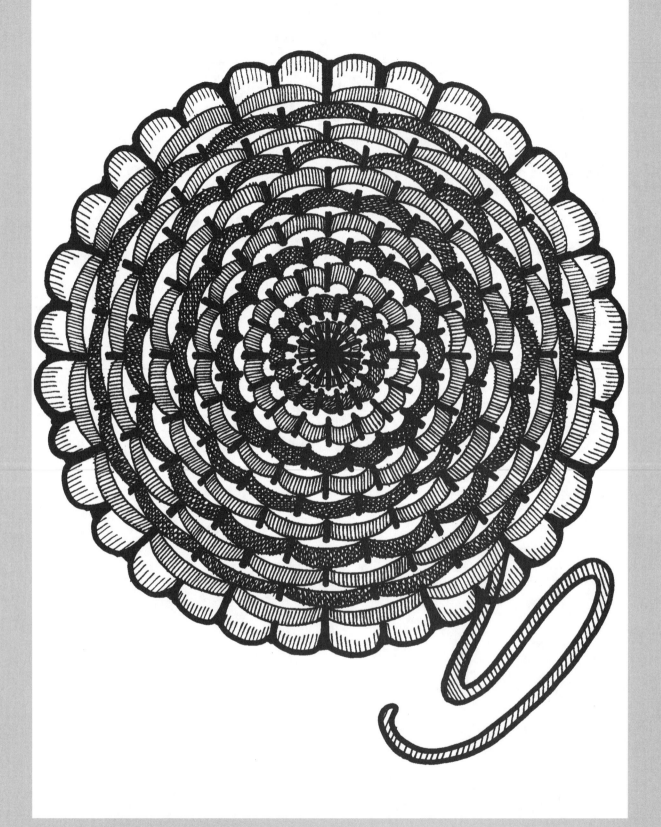

Circle Weaving

MATERIALS:

- cardboard (pulp paper plates may also be used)
- scissors
- pencil and eraser
- skein of yarn

- ballpoint pen
- compass
- ruler
- measuring tape
- masking tape

DIRECTIONS:

1. Draw an 8″ circle on your cardboard and cut it out to make a loom.

2. Using a measuring tape, mark lines that are ½″ long and that are ½″ apart all around the edge of the circle until you have 43 lines, as shown.

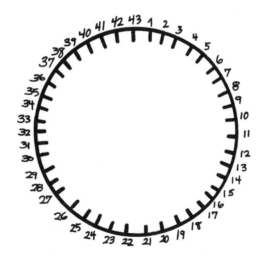

3. Cut the notches and label each with your pen from number 1 to number 43.

4. Tie a large knot in the end of a piece of yarn on a skein of yarn.

5. Do not cut the yarn.

6. Pull the end of a piece of yarn through notch number 1 so that it is in the back of the cardboard circle.

7. On the front of the circle, stretch the yarn tautly across the surface and pull it into notch number 22.

8. Wrap the yarn around the back of the circle and back through notch number 23 to the front of the circle.

143

9. Continue this procedure according to the pattern of numbers so that the yarn stretches only across the surface of the cardboard on the front and so that the loops around the notches are only on the back.

1 – 22 – 23 – 2 – 3 – 24 – 25 – 4 – 5 – 26 – 27 – 6 – 7 – 28 – 29 – 8 – 9 – 30 – 31 – 10 – 11 – 32 – 33 – 12 – 13 – 34 – 35 – 14 – 15 – 36 – 37 – 16 – 17 – 38 – 39 – 18 – 19 – 40 – 41 – 20 – 21 – 42 – 43

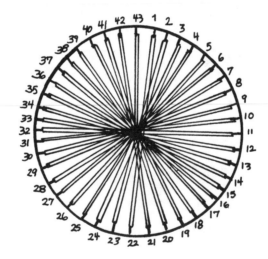

10. When you reach notch number 43, extend the yarn to the back of the circle and tape it in place with masking tape.

11. Thread a one-foot piece of yarn under the middle of your yarn design and tie in a double knot.

12. Take the other end and begin weaving at any point over and under the warp thread, pulling the yarn toward the center of your design. Continue in the same direction around the circle.

13. When this yarn runs out, tie another color or textured piece of yarn to this and continue weaving.

14. After you reach the edge of the circle, gently pull the yarn out of the notches and remove the masking tape from the end piece of the back.

15. Weave this piece into the weaving to become part of your design.

16. You may stretch the weaving out into the loops or attach fringe to each loop.

Paper Weaving

Paper Weaving

MATERIALS:

- **2 sheets of 12" x 18" construction paper: 1 red, 1 white**
- **glue or paste**
- **scissors**
- **pencil**
- **ruler**

DIRECTIONS:

1. Place one sheet of construction paper on top of the other and draw a line where they overlap.

2. Using this line as a base, draw a half circle which touches the top of your paper. Cut along the arc of your circle, and then use this cutout as a guide for creating the same shape on the other sheet of paper.

3. Using a ruler or a 1" strip as your guide, draw lines to divide the space below your baseline into equal strips; then cut along the lines. You can save time on this step by cutting through two sheets at once.

4. Now overlap strips as shown and begin to weave one into the other, one at a time.

5. After all the strips have been woven, the ends should be glued together on both sides.

Ojos de Dios

Ojos de Dios

MATERIALS:

- **yarn or colored string**
- **toothpicks, craft sticks, twigs, branches**
- **scissors**

DIRECTIONS:

1. Otherwise known as "God's Eyes," Ojos de Dios may be traced to the Indians of Mexico. They carried two shields, one in back and one in front, which were circular with a hole in the center to serve as the eye in a mask. They were thought of as representing a part of a god. Each pattern of colors was symbolic for a certain god.

2. Cross whichever two sticks you choose and wrap a few times with the string or yarn.

 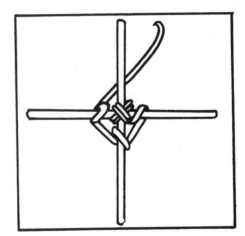

3. Then always in the same direction of rotation, the string should be brought around one stick, jumped to the next, wrapped around it, jumped to the next, and so on.

4. Change colors frequently.

5. Using three or four sticks that intersect in the center will make more complex patterns for older students.

6. It is also possible to make three-dimensional examples by inserting a stick at right angles to the basic plane with the weaving alternating between two planes.

7. For clusters of ojos built on a small branch, short sections of similar twigs may be tied in at right angles here and there to begin each "eye." Suspending other twig ojos from the branch by threads is effective.

Straw Weaving

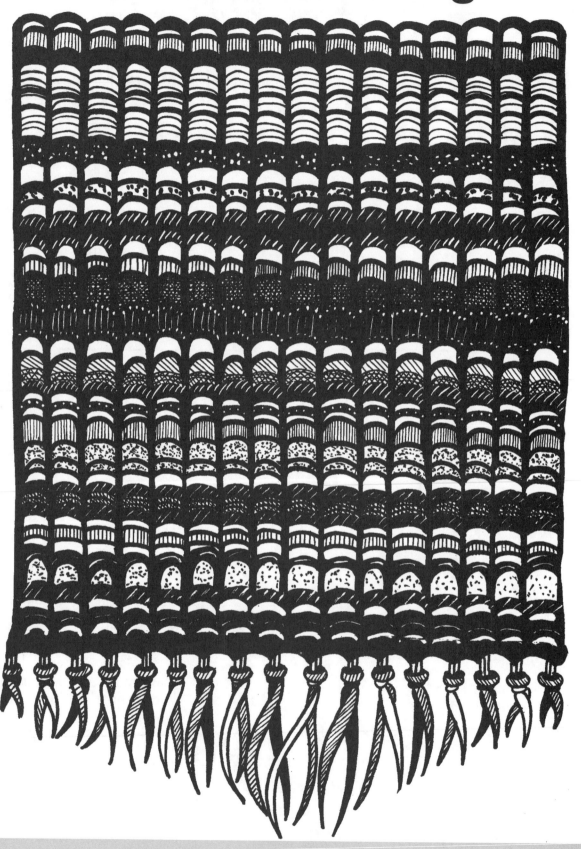

Straw Weaving

MATERIALS:

- **3 plastic drinking straws**
- **scissors**
- **yarn**
- **masking tape**
- **beads or shells with a hole cut in each**

DIRECTIONS:

1. Cut the straws in half and keep five of the halves.

2. Cut five pieces of yarn that are each four feet long.

3. Thread each warp thread separately through each straw, out the top, and overlap about ½" of it to the outside of the straw. Use a small piece of masking tape to smoothly wrap around and secure the yarn to the straw as shown. These are the warp threads.

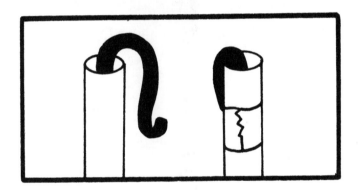

4. Make sure the tape is smooth, because rough edges will catch the yarn when you begin weaving.

5. Cut another piece of yarn about two feet long. Tie it to an end straw near the top and, holding the yarn in one hand and the five straws close together in the other, begin to pull it in and out of each straw near the top, weaving over one straw and under the next as shown. This will form the weft threads.

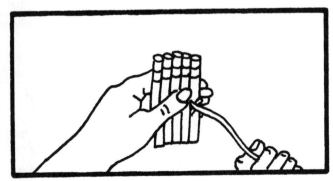

6. When you reach the end, loop the yarn around and weave back to where you began the same way: over one straw and under one as shown. Repeat.

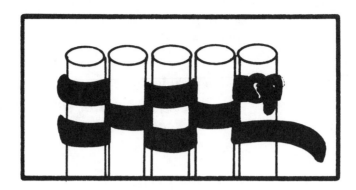

7. When you finish with this piece of yarn, tie it to another piece of yarn and continue.

8. Beads or shells can be threaded through your piece of weaving yarn at any point and can then be woven right into your design.

9. As the tops of your straws fill up with weaving, you will need to gently push some of the weaving downward, but never let all of the weaving slip off the straws or there will be a gap in your weaving and it will be difficult to start again.

10. If you are making a belt, when it is long enough to go around your waist, remove the tape from the yarn at the top of the straws and discard the tape. Pull off the straws and discard them.

11. Carefully ease the woven part down the strands until it is in the center.

12. Using all strands of yarn at the ends, tie a knot in each one right up against the weaving to keep it from moving.

13. Repeat at the other end.

14. Beads or shells can be tied to the ends of the fringe if desired.

15. You can also divide the weaving by weaving only over and under the first three straws on either side for making different colored sections.

16. To add interest to your weaving, add new warp threads to the warp in the original weaving and thread straws on the new warp. *Weave* as before and, again, remove straws when the weaving is completed.

17. If you are making a person, different sections can be sewn together. Features can be woven in, or you may fashion them from cut pieces of yarn or felt and glue them on.

Crafts

LEVEL 1

Stuffed Butterflies is a lesson in creating larger-than-life, three-dimensional paper objects. It is an opportunity for students to think big, and to simply enjoy the unrestrictive nature of work done on a grand scale. In the suggested group activity, *Planetary Achitecture,* students are asked to create a three-dimensional environmental landscape using a variety of found materials. Architecture is later introduced when students add appropriate structures to their newly created environments.

LEVEL 2

Point-to-Point Yarn Pictures is an activity that allows students to create interesting designs with yarn when they stretch it between nails that have been attached to a wooden base. *Soft Foam Masks* are created by cutting, arranging, and attaching colorful foam shapes together. *Constructional Problem Solving* presents the challenge of building a piece of sculpture using a wide variety of objects and forms. *Complete the Picture* is an activity that uses a magazine photo to spark the imagination and to serve as a starting point for a new composition.

LEVEL 3

Wood Sculpture introduces assemblage techniques and also provides students with a new medium to explore. *Hand Puppets* introduce new puppetry techniques, including modeling with plastered gauze, increased characterization, and more elaborate costume design. *Aluminum Plaster Casting* introduces plaster as a medium and casting as a process, as well as techniques for creating metal molds. *Metal Masks* further explores the mask as an art form as well as further exploring the techniques involved in tooling a metal surface.

Stuffed Butterflies

Complete the Picture

Hand Puppets

Stuffed Butterflies

Stuffed Butterflies

MATERIALS:

- pencil and eraser
- 2 large heavy pieces of 36" x 48" paper
- newspaper
- tempera paints and brushes
- stapler
- masking tape
- heavy string

DIRECTIONS:

1. View slides or pictures of butterflies.

2. Draw a simple-shaped butterfly.

3. Include simple designs repeated on each wing.

4. Transfer the drawing to one 36" x 48" paper.

5. Paint in designs and paint the outline around the edge.

6. When dry, flip it over onto another piece of paper. Trace carefully around the drawing, which you should hold in place with masking tape. Cut out the second butterfly drawing and flip it over.

7. Draw identical butterfly designs on this side and paint.

8. When dry, put the two sides together with the painted side facing outward. Begin to staple the two sides together, but leave an opening about two feet long, which you should stuff lightly with crushed newspaper. Then, finish your stapling.

9. Holes can be punched in the top of each wing in order to hang the butterfly with heavy string.

Planetary Architecture

Planetary Architecture

MATERIALS:

- large cardboard box
- craft knife
- plaster-impregnated gauze
- newspaper
- construction paper scraps
- glazed paper
- yarn
- silver glitter
- sand
- sawdust
- aluminum foil
- colored acetate
- Styrofoam
- sugar cubes
- India ink
- chalk
- crayons
- tempera paints and brushes
- various glues

DIRECTIONS:

1. You are a space explorer and have just landed for a rest on the uninhabited planet "Lambor." You need to have a shelter that will protect you from moondust but that will also allow you to look out and watch the sky as stars and spaceships whirl by and to observe the planet.

2. Carefully remove one side of your box and begin constructing your landscape by arranging crumpled mounds of newspaper in the bottom of the box. These newspaper hills and valleys should then be covered with overlapping layers of gauze. When dry, use paint to decorate the landscape. Other materials can be used as well; perhaps glitter for your mountain peaks, sand for your deserts, or sawdust for your canyons.

3. Next, using cardboard or Styrofoam, design and construct your shelter. Attach this to your landscape with glue.

4. Preparations must be made for buildings for visitors to make them feel welcome, comfortable, and happy. See if any other buildings are necessary for the needs of the community.

5. Tape a piece of colored acetate across the opening in the box when you have finished building.

Point-to-Point
Yarn Designs

Point-to-Point Yarn Designs

MATERIALS:

- **yarn**
- **scissors**
- **3 to 5 pieces of wood of various lengths**
- **nails and hammer**
- **1" brads—small nails or staples for use with wood**
- **cardboard box**
- **straight pins**
- **liquid starch**

DIRECTIONS:

1. Take the lengths of wood and arrange a frame for the web, which will be irregular in shape. Nail them together by overlapping the edges.

2. Nail the brads onto the edge of this wood frame. These brads do not need to be evenly spaced. Hammer them about halfway in, so that the yarn can be fastened to the part sticking up. The irregularity of the shape of the frame and the uneven spacing of the brads help make an interesting design.

3. If a cardboard box is used, pins can be stuck to its edges.

4. Begin by tying the end of the yarn to one of the brads or pins.

5. Loop the yarn from one brad to another and from one side to another in what you consider to be an interesting design.

6. When finished, fasten the end of the yarn by wetting it with glue or liquid starch and pasting the end to another piece of yarn in the design.

7. Soak the completed yarn design in liquid starch.

8. When dry, remove the yarn design from the frame.

Soft Foam Masks

Soft Foam Masks

MATERIALS:

- **foam carpet padding (purchase in rolls or collect scraps from a carpet company)**
- **heavy-duty scissors or snips**
- **contact cement or white glue**
- **stapler**
- **string, yarn, fabric, and so forth**

A **mask** is a decorative covering for the face. Masks have been used for thousands of years for a variety of purposes including: to prepare for hunting, for religious ceremonies, for superstitious healing, and for decoration. Today, we see masks on children at Halloween, masks painted on clowns' faces, on actors' faces, and so forth. In museums, we can see examples of Native American Indian, African, Eskimo, and theatrical masks. These masks are made of wood, clay, papier-mâché, and other materials.

DIRECTIONS:

1. Masks may be used for fun and for decoration, such as Mardi Gras and Halloween, and for more serious reasons, such as before a hunt or to ward off evil spirits from someone who is sick. Your mask will be just for fun.

2. Experiment by cutting, connecting, and forming various pieces of the foam.

3. Try twisting, layering, intertwining, and cutting through the foam sheets to achieve special effects.

4. When you think you have control of the foam, cut and form a head cover.

5. Once a comfortable cover or cap is achieved, develop features by cutting into the foam for eye holes, ears, nose, and mouth.

6. Add to the basic features in a manner that enhances the mask's decorative and expressive qualities.

7. Is your mask wearable? well crafted? expressive?

Constructional Problem Solving

Constructional Problem Solving

MATERIALS:

- **balsa wood strips** $\frac{1}{16}$**" thick**
- **sharp scissors**
- **cardboard**
- **block of Styrofoam**
- **glue**

- **craft sticks or tongue depressors**
- **tempera paints and brushes**
- **egg carton cups**
- **paper straws**

DIRECTIONS:

Part I

1. Glue Styrofoam to cardboard to form a base for the sculpture.

2. Cut out shapes in balsa wood.

3. Use large, medium, and small shapes.

4. Vary the shapes of each.

5. Try building up layers of balsa wood for a three-dimensional effect.

6. Glue some pieces and stick into the Styrofoam base.

7. Let dry and paint.

8. Add to these pieces, designing higher and wider.

9. Turn the base around as you work to be sure that it is interesting from all sides.

Part II

Do the same as above using egg carton cups.

Part III

Do the same as above using paper straws. (You have now experienced three construction problems including line, flat shapes, and three-dimensional shapes.)

Complete the Picture

Complete the Picture

MATERIALS:

- **12" x 18" manila paper**
- **magazines**
- **scissors and paste or glue**
- **crayons or markers**

DIRECTIONS:

1. Cut out an object that is not a person or an animal from a magazine.

2. Glue it onto the manila paper.

3. Using your crayons or markers, complete an entire picture adding other objects, people, animals, or buildings to tell a story and to make your picture interesting to look at and out of the ordinary.

Wood Sculpture

Wood Sculpture

MATERIALS:

- **small wood parts usually used for toys**
- **white glue or water-soluble wood glue**
- **markers**
- **yarn and fabric**
- **craft sticks or tongue depressors**
- **spools**
- **other small wood pieces**
- **12" x 18" pieces of chipboard**
- **masking tape**

DIRECTIONS:

1. Look at the shapes of the wood and think about what can be made from them. Does one remind you of a headlight, a hat, a head, or a wheel?

2. Begin gluing various parts together. You might form cars, comic people, robots, airplanes, or furniture.

3. Think of an environment where your first object could be. Could it be an automobile race, a rock concert, a department store, or a place to eat?

4. Build more parts together to form other objects or people for your environment and glue them onto the chipboard.

5. Masking tape will hold stubborn pieces together until they dry.

6. Color may be added with markers.

7. Clothes and hair may be added with fabric and yarn.

8. The chipboard may also be colored with markers as part of the environment.

Hand Puppets

Hand Puppets

MATERIALS:

- **plaster-impregnated gauze**
- **old scissors**
- **warm water**
- **newspaper**
- **felt**
- **sharp scissors**
- **chalk**
- **yarn**
- **notions: rickrack, lace, ribbon, buttons, and so forth**
- **tempera paints and brushes**
- **cotton**
- **fake fur**
- **masking tape**
- **oaktag**
- **gloss acrylic polymer**

DIRECTIONS:

1. Roll up a single sheet of newspaper into a round shape.

2. Roll this up inside another single sheet of newspaper. Squeeze into a good round shape and secure with masking tape.

3. Cut a piece of oaktag 3″ x 1″; roll it loosely around your "pointing" finger and secure with tape.

4. Tape this to the head to form the neck as shown.

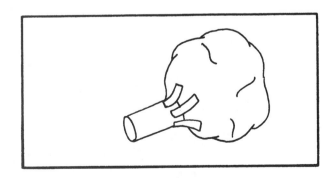

5. Tape on features for your puppet's face, which can be made by cutting oaktag shapes or squeezing or rolling a newspaper shape until it looks like the character you want to make. Exaggerate the size of all features.

6. You can add hats, chins, cheeks, ears, noses, mouths, teeth, or whatever you like as shown.

7. Cut small pieces of gauze with your old scissors, dip in warm water, and begin to layer on your puppet's head, neck, and all other features, overlapping each piece for strength until you have completely covered your puppet.

8. Use your finger dipped in water to smooth out each piece and also to release the plaster to fill in the holes.

9. Let dry.

10. Paint with tempera, let dry, and coat with polymer.

11. Glue on yarn, raffia, or cotton if necessary.

12. Lay your hand on a piece of felt as shown.

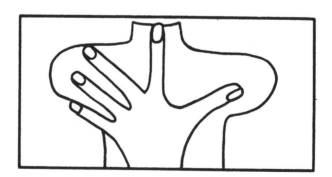

13. Use the chalk to trace around your hand in order to make a pattern for the costume as shown.

14. Cut this out, lay on another piece of felt, trace around your first felt pattern, and cut this out.

15. Use glue to fasten the two pieces together, leaving open the neck and bottom so that your hand can slip in.

16. Let dry.

17. Glue the neck inside the neck hole and tape until dry. Remove the tape.

18. Glue buttons, lace, fur, and so forth on the costume if desired.

Aluminum
Plaster Casting

Aluminum Plaster Casting

MATERIALS:

- pipe cleaner
- 4" x 6" manila paper
- newspaper
- 9" x 12" aluminum tooling foil
- pencils or tongue depressor
- plaster
- masking tape
- tempera paint and brushes
- sandpaper
- ruler

DIRECTIONS:

1. Begin by sketching your idea on a sheet of manila 4" x 6".

2. Next, fold masking tape around the edges of a 9" x 12" sheet of aluminum tooling foil. Then, center your drawing on top of the foil and secure it with a piece of tape.

3. Place a small stack of newspapers under the foil to act as a cushion.

4. Transfer your drawing from the manila paper to the foil by drawing over your outlines and remembering to press hard with your pencil.

5. When the transfer is complete, remove your drawing and begin embossing or tooling the foil by pushing some parts out and others in. This can be done with a dull pencil or tongue depressor. You can decorate and texturize the surface of the foil by using a sharper pencil and adding various patterns and markings.

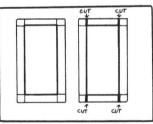
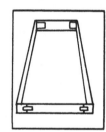

6. Next, use a ruler to outline four equal margins and cut along the lines indicated. Then fold up the corners and tape in place as shown.

7. Now the plaster can be mixed and poured. While it is setting, place a pipe cleaner shaped like this (see drawing on right) in the plaster. When your casting is dry, this will serve as a hanger.

8. After removing the hardened plaster casting from the aluminum, you may wish to use sandpaper on any rough edges.

9. Now you are ready to complete your work by painting it.

Metal Masks

Metal Masks

MATERIALS:

- 9" x 12" paper
- 9" x 12" piece of aluminum foil
- pencil and eraser
- masking tape
- newspaper
- craft sticks or pencil-thin dowels cut to pencil length
- markers that will adhere to metal

DIRECTIONS:

1. View slides or photos of masks made by Native American Indians and Eskimos.

2. Masks were used for religious and hunting ceremonies and for curing sickness, as well as for decoration.

3. Draw the outside shape of a face for your mask and include some type of ears.

4. Add unusually shaped eyes, nose, and mouth, keeping in mind whether you want to create a comedic or a frightening mask.

5. Add simple shapes to the forehead, cheeks, and chin.

6. Tape your drawing onto the 9" x 12" piece of foil and lay this on a pad of newspapers at least 2" thick.

7. Trace over all the pencil lines by pressing hard enough with a pencil so that the lines are transferred to the foil.

8. Remove the drawing and begin to tool, or press down, inside the entire area of the nose using the craft sticks or dowels.

9. Flip the foil over and tool inside the entire area of the next space outward from the nose.

10. Flip over the foil and continue in the next area to tool so that the area is pressed out in one direction and the area next to it is tooled out in the opposite direction. (One area pops forward and the other area recedes.)

11. When all areas are tooled either forward or back, turn the side up where the nose "pops" forward and outline all shapes in black marker.

12. Fill in some of the shapes with markers of other colors so that you achieve a balance between the foil color and the marker colors.

13. The mask may be punched with holes at the top in order to hang it, or it may be stapled onto paper or cardboard for display.

PART II

ART ACTIVITIES FOR THE INTERMEDIATE GRADES

Section I

Drawing

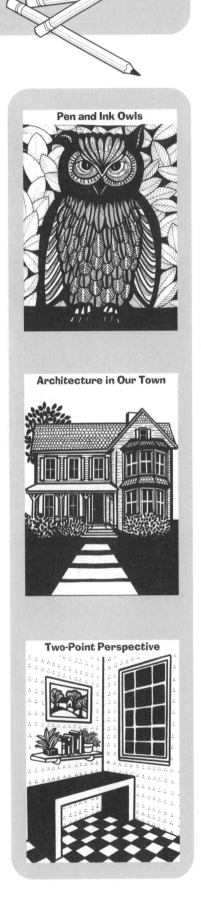

Pen and Ink Owls

Architecture in Our Town

Two-Point Perspective

LEVEL 4

In *Action Figures,* further emphasis on body proportion and movement of the body are brought into play using basic geometric ovals and circles. The art medium of pen and ink is introduced in *Pen and Ink Owls,* while different parts are textured, shaded, stippled, cross-hatched, and otherwise experimented with, using pen and ink techniques. In *Two-Pencil Drawings,* the student holds two pencils in one hand and creates a random design. Together with the technique of shading, this lesson demonstrates three-dimensional representation in drawing. The concept of still life is introduced in *Musical Still Life* and the composition of objects, reinforcing the use of overlapping, is studied as is further work on proportion. *Personality Profiles* explores the concept of the silhouetted profile and of drawing objects based on aspects of each individual's personality.

LEVEL 5

Window Views emphasizes distance, depth, foreground, middle, and background pictorial elements as well as the concepts that objects appear smaller as they recede in space and that dark colors show distance and light colors show closeness. Facial features and proportions are studied in *Half-Face Portraits* fantasy is given further exploration and in *Whale Dreams.* Advanced observation of architectural techniques and a beginning awareness of perspective play a primary role in *Architecture in Our Town.*

LEVEL 6

Portraiture studies the proportion of facial features and their placement in a portrait. Further study in perspective on a more formal scale is conducted in *Two-Point Perspective.* In *Bicycle Drawings* detail and proportion, as well as close observation, come into play. *Texture Drawings* reinforces the use of textural elements as an integral part of designing and adding interest. *Idiomatic Illustrations* looks at some commonly used expression in a new light.

Action Figures

Action Figures

MATERIALS:

- **pencil and eraser**
- **drawing paper**
- **markers and crayons**

DIRECTIONS:

1. One way to make drawing people a little easier is to think of the body as a series of simple shapes joined together.

2. To begin, ask someone to be your model. Ask this person to "freeze" in action, perhaps pretending to be swinging a bat or running or stretching. Any "action" pose will do.

3. Since it is very difficult for the model to hold such a pose for long, you will have to work quickly.

4. Begin by sketching a stick figure with your pencil. Show the direction of the head, a bend in an arm, the tilt of the hips, and so forth. This sketch should be *very* simple, and your model should relax as soon as you've finished it. See example A.

5. The next step is to "fill out" your stick figure. See example B.

6. The last step (example C) is to outline your new form carefully and add clothes. Afterward, you can erase your inside guidelines and "color in" your person.

7. A field trip to a gym class would be a helpful activity to include with this project.

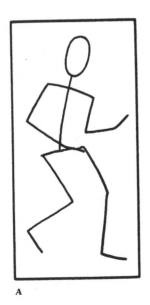

A   B   C

Pen and Ink Owls

Pen and Ink Owls

MATERIALS:

- newspaper
- drawing ink and steel nibbed pens or a variety of thin felt markers
- 9" x 12" white drawing paper
- pencil
- scrap paper

DIRECTIONS:

1. Begin by spreading newspaper under your drawing paper. This is very important because some drawing inks are permanent and can stain your working surface. Needless to say, you should be careful when working with inks not to spill them or let them spatter or drip.

2. After setting up, sketch your owl on white drawing paper. Try to make it large. Fill in as much detail as possible with your pencil.

3. Now dip your pen in the drawing ink and wipe it against the inside of the bottle as you remove it, so that it won't drip. On a piece of scrap paper, experiment with some of the different line types you can use to make an interesting drawing. See the following examples.

See if you can invent some new styles.

4. Now begin to fill in the owl. Try to use the widest variety of strokes possible. You may wish to add an interesting background.

Two-Pencil Drawings

Two-Pencil Drawings

MATERIALS:

- newsprint or practice paper
- 1 sheet of white 12" x 18" construction paper
- 2 pencils and an eraser
- crayons and markers

DIRECTIONS:

1. These drawings are fun to make but will take a little practice on a piece of newsprint paper.

2. Start by holding two pencils in your right or left hand (whichever you normally draw with) as shown in the illustration. Keep your hand very stiff and upright. While you are getting the feel for it, try "dragging" your pencils across the paper in different directions. It is important that you apply equal pressure to both pencils as you draw.

3. After some practice you can begin to try curves, loops, and circles.

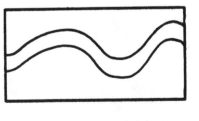

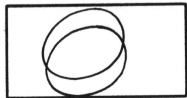

You may even want to write your name.

4. By now you've noticed how your pencils create a double image. In order to use this to its best advantage in creating a design, you may need to fill in the double image as if it were a solid ribbon with black on one side and white on the other.

Before

After

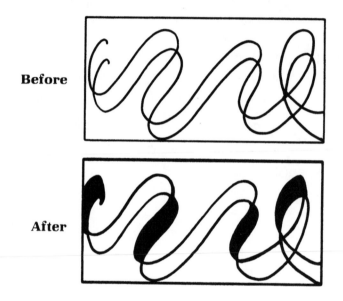

5. Use your new skill to create a picture or design.

6. If you can't quite get the hang of using both pencils in one hand, you can achieve the same result by taping the two pencils together and drawing with them as if they were one.

Musical Still Life

Musical Still Life

MATERIALS:

- **manila paper**
- **musical instruments**
- **12" x 18" white drawing paper**
- **pencil and eraser**
- **thin black permanent marker**
- **watercolors and brushes**

A **still life** is a picture representing objects, such as fruits and flowers, that are neither moving nor alive. Still-life studies have been used by artists as a subject for hundreds of years because they can be composed of items an artist can find right in his or her home. Also, many techniques of art, such as shading, overlapping, proportion, and composition, can all be practiced using a still life. Representing different surfaces, such as glass, metal, and wood, are easily practiced in a still life using different lines, textures, and shading.

DIRECTIONS:

1. Very often things that we imagine will be difficult to draw become simplified after observing them closely.

2. Start by creating a very detailed drawing of an instrument—any instrument. Make it large enough to fill your sheet of manila paper. When it is completed, set it aside.

3. Set up a still life or an arrangement of musical instruments in such a way that you can see them from your drawing position. Any type of instrument will do, from harmonicas to saxophones. Students who take music lessons often bring their instruments to school and may be able to provide you with your models.

4. Spend some time just looking at the composition of instruments and at the arrangement of the shapes they present.

5. Next, begin to sketch what you see. You may wish to show only one or two instruments from the arrangement and draw them in great detail. Or, you may want to sketch the overall composition of all the instruments with less emphasis on individual detail.

6. When your drawing is completed, outline it with a thin, permanent, black marker and paint it carefully with watercolors.

Personality Profiles

Personality Profiles

MATERIALS:

- **1 sheet black 12" x 18" construction paper**
- **1 sheet white 12" x 18" construction paper**
- **scissors**
- **white glue**
- **pencils or markers**
- **tape and light source**

DIRECTIONS:

1. To begin, you will need to cut out a silhouette of your profile. Find a strong light in your work area and place it in such a way that it casts a shadow of your profile on the wall.

2. Tape the white construction paper to the wall in the spot where your shadow appeared. Now ask a friend to trace the shadow of your profile onto the paper.

3. Afterward, remove the white paper from the wall and place the black paper beneath it. Then, following your outline, cut through both sheets of paper.

4. This will give you two identical profiles. Use the white one to show things about yourself—things you like to do, places you like to go, things that you think about, dreams that you may have. These will show people not just how you look but also who you are.

5. When you are finished coloring in your drawings, place this white profile on top of the black one, allowing the black one to protrude a bit in order to emphasize your profile.

Window Views

Window Views

MATERIALS:

- **tempera paints and brushes**
- **markers**
- **pencils and erasers**
- **rules**
- **1 sheet of 12" x 18" manila**

DIRECTIONS:

1. The object of this type of picture is to use as many pictorial devices as possible in order to create the illusion of depth. To begin, choose a window—any type of window—such as a store window, a windshield, a porthole, or even the cracked window of a haunted house.

2. Outline your basic window shape and include as many details as possible, such as molding, glass panes, shutters, curtains, latches, and so forth.

3. Next, begin to draw the scene visible from your window. This might include hills and valleys, oceans and ships, stars and planets, or the contents of a shop.

4. Whatever you draw, remember to make things smaller and smaller as they get farther and farther away from your window. Some things will overlap; this helps us see what things are in front of other things.

5. Now you are ready to show things that are in front of your window: a person looking out the window, a cat on the window sill, a hanging plant, a chair or other furniture, wallpaper, paints on the wall, and so forth. Remember that the more detail you add, the more convincing your picture will be.

6. Finally, paint your pictures using cool colors (blue, green, gray, purple) to make some parts recede and warm colors (orange, yellow, red, brown) to make other parts come forward.

Half-Face Portraits

Half-Face Portraits

MATERIALS:

- **ruler**
- **magazines**
- **pencil and eraser**
- **9" x 12" drawing paper**
- **scissors**
- **glue**

DIRECTIONS:

1. Look through a magazine for a large, full-face photo. Carefully cut it out of the magazine.

2. Next, use a ruler to draw a line down the middle of the face; then cut along this line.

3. Trim any outer edges or advertising from the photo; then glue it on one side of your paper.

4. Now fill in the missing half of the face, matching the features by studying the photo. Use your pencil to create shadows and highlights. This will make the face appear to be three-dimensional.

Whale Dreams

Whale Dreams

MATERIALS:

- **pencil and eraser**
- **12" x 18" white paper**
- **thin black marker**

DIRECTIONS:

1. Think of the dreams you have had—perhaps doing something you couldn't or wouldn't do in real life.
2. Draw what you think a whale might dream.
3. You may include several scenes, overlapping in different sections of your paper.
4. Try to think of a fantasy to include in the dream that a whale might have, such as flying, being a ship for people to ride on, and so forth.
5. Try to include a nightmare portion. Think of what a whale might fear.
6. Trace over all the lines with the marker and color in certain parts for emphasis.
7. Try to include a drawing of the whale.
8. If there are any empty spaces between portions, draw in various repeated patterns, such as stars, stripes, spirals, and zigzags, and fill these in or outline them in marker.

Architecture in Our Town

Architecture in Our Town

MATERIALS:

- **12" x 18" white drawing paper**
- **pencil and eraser**
- **photos of architecturally interesting houses in your town**

Architecture is the art of building, and it includes the design, construction, and decorative treatment that give a building a certain character or style. American architecture has gone through many stylistic periods, including the English style of Jamestown and of Plymouth, the formal periods of the Georgian, the Federal, and the Greek Revival eras, the simplicity of the New England saltbox, the log cabin of the westward expansion, the Victorian Era, and modern design beginning with the architect Frank Lloyd Wright.

The Georgian style is balanced and often features fanlighted doorways. Such doorways are sometimes pillared, pedimented, and graced with a Palladian window above and a hip roof.

The Federal period shows more ornamentation to a "monitor roof" to light the stairwell. The windows are often larger, sometimes reaching to the floor.

The Greek Revival house often has a portico with columns.

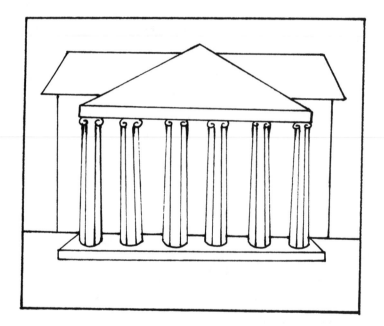

The Victorian house often has wooden "gingerbread" work, cast-iron tracery, patterned shingling, intricate brickwork, and other more lavish decoration than before.

See if you can locate some of these parts in the house you have chosen and identify its period.

DIRECTIONS:

1. Remember, in drawing architecture, all vertical lines remain vertical; it is only the horizontal lines that slant.

2. Keep in mind that as an object gets farther away from you, it appears smaller.

3. Study the photo you chose and notice these principles.

4. Draw the photo, including all of the details and using the principles mentioned earlier.

5. Shade in certain areas to give emphasis and contrast to your drawing.

6. Include bushes, walks, and part of the lawn to provide a "base" for the house.

Portraiture

Portraiture

MATERIALS:

- **pencil and eraser**   • **paper**   • **ruler**

Portraiture is the art of creating a likeness of a person. Pictures that an artist paints of him- or herself are called self-portraits. Rembrandt van Rijn, one of the world's most famous artists, was a great portraitist. During his lifetime, he created many penetrating portraits of different people and more than 100 self-portraits. These self-portraits show him at various ages and in different moods, and they all help to tell us the story of his life.

DIRECTIONS:

1. Begin by drawing a large oval.
2. Measure the length of your oval and draw a horizontal line at the halfway point.
3. Now measure the length of this line and divide the length into five equal sections.

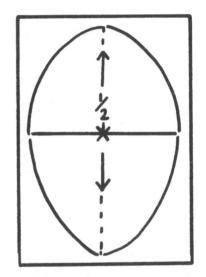

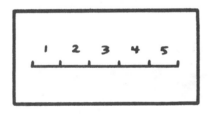

4. Divide the same length in half and draw a line extending from the forehead to the chin.
5. Extend the lines to the right and left of your center line from the forehead to the chin.

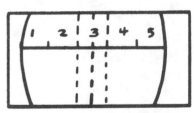

6. Now measure the distance from your horizontal line to the chin and find the halfway point. Draw a horizontal line at this point.
7. Next, measure the distance from this line to the chin and draw another horizontal line at the halfway point.
8. Now that all of your guidelines are complete, use them to determine the correct placement of your subject's features.
9. After you have drawn all of the features, you can erase your guidelines and use your pencil to do shading and modeling.

Two-Point Perspective

Two-Point Perspective

MATERIALS:

- **12" x 18" paper**
- **pencil and eraser**

Perspective is the art of showing on a flat surface various objects, architecture, or landscape in such a way as to simulate (that is, give the illusion of) dimension and space between objects near and far away.

DIRECTIONS:

1. Draw a line from side to side on your paper slightly below the middle as shown.

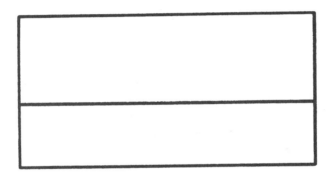

2. This is called the horizon line and represents where the sky meets the ground.

3. Place two Xs on this line near the sides as shown.

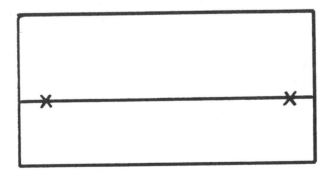

4. These are called the vanishing points.

5. Draw a vertical line between the Xs as shown on the next page and connect the Xs to the ends of the line.

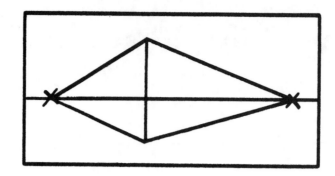

6. Now you can draw a building using your lines as shown in the illustration. The windows follow the same angles or lines.

7. These angles to the building and windows are optical illusions. You know that a building doesn't really slant like this, but it does look like this *because* objects appear smaller as they go back in space. A train track is a good example. It looks like art "A," not like art "B."

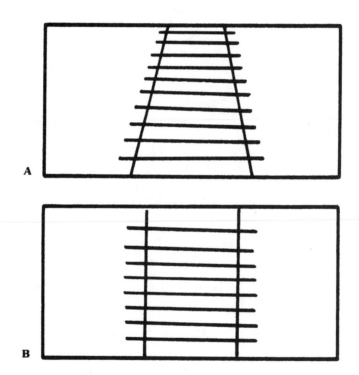

8. Now you are going to pick a corner of the room to draw. Pick an interesting corner with lots of objects and some furniture. A corner of a kitchen is a good choice.

9. If you draw it as shown in the following illustration, remember that the invisible dotted lines going back to the vanishing points still exist. Do not draw these in.

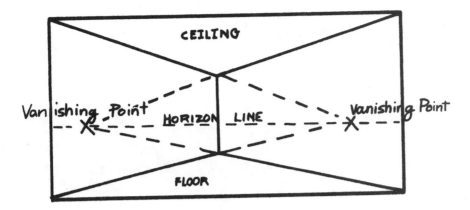

10. All the angles of tables, chairs, and pictures on the wall follow the angles of the floor and ceiling.

11. Remember all vertical lines will remain completely vertical; it is only the horizontal lines that angle or slant.

Bicycle Drawings

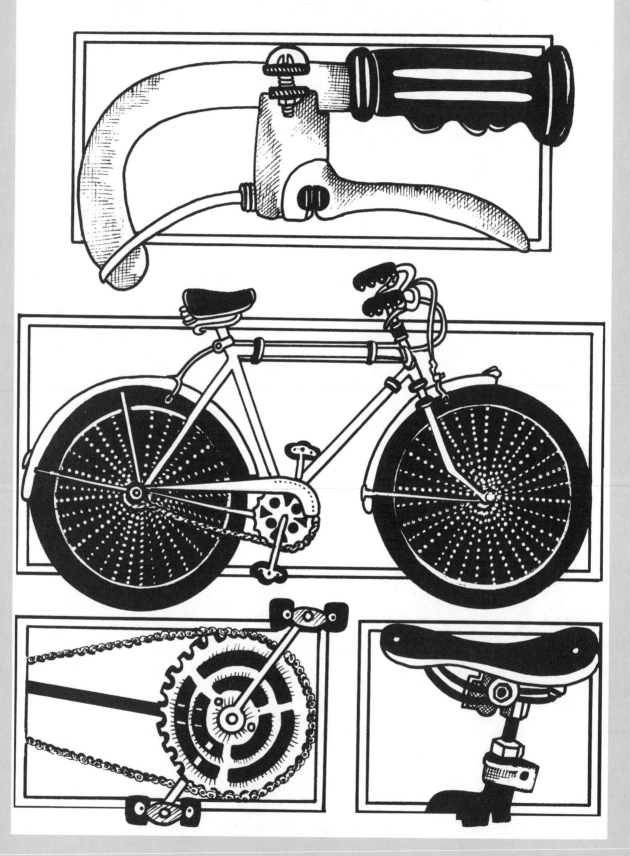

Bicycle Drawings

MATERIALS:

- 1 two-wheeled bicycle
- 12" x 18" white paper
- magnifying glass (optional)
- pencil and eraser
- thin black marker

DIRECTIONS:

1. Set up a two-wheeled bicycle on a table so that you are viewing it directly from its side and can see both wheels.

2. Lightly draw two large circles on your paper where you think the wheels would be.

3. Remember to draw large enough so that the bike will fill the space of the paper.

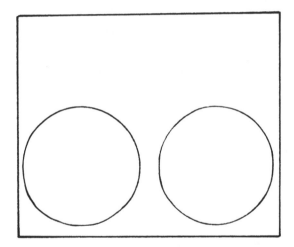 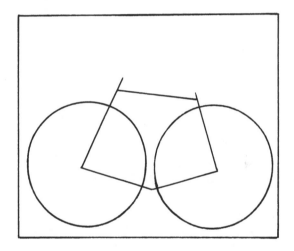

4. Study the angles of the main frame or bars of the bike and draw these lines in lightly.

5. Carefully observe the position of the handlebars, and draw them exactly as they appear. If one side of the handlebar obscures your view of the other side, simply draw the side you see.

6. Begin to sketch in the more detailed sections of the bike, the seat, the chain, pedals, fenders, and so forth.

7. Trace over all the pencil lines with a marker.

8. Erase any visible pencil lines.

9. As a follow-up exercise, try focusing on and magnifying one part of the bicycle and turning it into an exciting nonobjective drawing.

Texture Drawings

Texture Drawings

MATERIALS:

- **pencil and eraser**
- **9" x 12" white drawing paper**
- **black thin marker**

DIRECTIONS:

1. Examine natural objects—such as tree bark, corn husks, rocks, and insects' wings—for their textural qualities. Notice how textural patterns can be used to emphasize and contrast forms and space.

2. Study photos or slides of insects. Notice the body parts and the segments of the legs.

3. Draw an insect very lightly with a pencil and make your drawing large enough so that some parts extend off the paper. Essential details of the insect should be put into your drawing.

4. Outline your drawing with a black thin marker.

5. Divide the negative space (the space around the "positive" space) within the insect with light pencil lines to provide background shapes.

6. This breakup of the negative space gives the picture interest and variety.

7. With the marker, make patterns within these spaces.

8. This will develop many interesting designs, which will be striking in black and white and will emphasize the difference between positive and negative spaces.

Idiomatic Illustrations

Idiomatic Illustrations

MATERIALS:

- 18" x 24" white drawing paper
- pencil and eraser
- thin black marker
- crayons

Idiomatic expressions are unique phrases that say one thing but mean something else. Confused? Take a look at the picture that accompanies this activity. This picture illustrates a commonly used idiomatic phrase. Can you guess what that phrase is? The picture shows us what the phrase *says,* but it does not show us what the phrase *means.* Do you know what the phrase means?

DIRECTIONS:

1. See how many other idiomatic phrases you can add to this list.

    a. Your eyes are bigger than your stomach.

    b. You're the apple of my eye.

    c. Cat got your tongue?

    d. I'm so hungry I could eat a horse.

    e. Catch a tiger by the tail.

2. Select one or two phrases and see if you can illustrate them. Use a pencil to complete your drawing, and then outline your pencil drawing with a thin, black marker. Color with crayon if you wish.

3. When you're finished, see if someone else can guess your idiomatic phrase just by looking at the picture.

Section II
Painting

LEVEL 4

Foil Clowns presents the technique of painting on aluminum foil and reemphasizes the use of pattern and repetition. In *Window Portraits,* the use of portraiture and the proportion of features is further explored. The technique of "crayon resist" is examined in *Jungle Resist,* which affords the opportunity to create intricate designs and further expands on the use of fluorescent colors.

LEVEL 5

Pointillism introduces the nineteenth-century impressionist concept and the use of a tool other than a brush with which to produce a stippling technique. Also emphasized is how colors placed close together blend at a distance. *Sand Paintings* explores a different medium for painting. In *Warm and Cool Colors,* the "temperature" of a painting is explored.

LEVEL 6

Use of shades and tints of one color is presented in *Monochromatic Painting* as well as continued compositional exercise. In *Multimedia Slides,* various solutions and found objects are used with all the elements of design in art to construct a small-scale composition that can be projected onto a screen.

Jungle Resist

Pointillism

Monochromatic Painting

Foil Clowns

Foil Clowns

MATERIALS:

- aluminum foil
- tempera paints and brushes
- one sheet of 12" x 18" manila paper
- masking tape
- liquid dish detergent
- pictures of clowns (from magazines, books, etc.)

DIRECTIONS:

1. Begin by looking at pictures of clowns. Notice how many geometric shapes can be found in their faces, hats, and costumes.

2. Tear off one sheet of foil a little larger than your manila paper.

3. Next, fold the excess foil back over the edges of the manila paper and tape it to keep it in place.

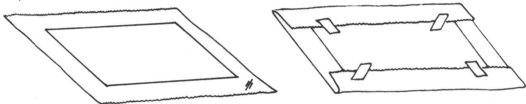

4. Start by drawing a large circle in the middle of your foil. Use the "wrong" end of the paintbrush to make your outline.

5. Next, place a large triangle on top of your circle and an oval around the bottom of it.

6. Next, see how many times a circle can be used to create features on your clown, such as eyes, nose, cheeks, and an open mouth, or polka dots and a pompom for the hat.

7. Add ears and hair and use a continuous line to create a collar inside your oval shape.

8. When all your outlining is done, begin to go over your outline with paint. A few drops of detergent should be added to the paint in order to make it adhere to the foil. Fluorescent paint can look particularly good because it is so bright.

9. Painting outlines rather than "filling-in" will make the best use of your foil background. Also, by painting patterns or designs within these outlined shapes, you can create a shimmering quality in your work.

Window Portraits

Window Portraits

MATERIALS:

- newspaper, sponges, water, brushes
- black tempera paint
- 2 drops of liquid dish detergent
- student models
- paper towels

DIRECTIONS:

1. Student models are led outside and are then asked to stand in front of windows where they can be viewed by the students in the classroom.

2. Next, cover the floor or counter space directly in front of each window with newspaper and equip each artist with a paper cup of black tempera, a thin brush, and a sponge. Liquid detergent should be stirred into the tempera for two reasons: (1) to help the paint adhere to the surface of the window, and (2) to simplify the cleanup of any paints that may spill. Please note that too much liquid detergent may make the paint crackle and blister after it dries, so add detergent sparingly.

3. Now, begin by asking your models to freeze in one position. (Having them stare at a fixed point will help them to remain still.) Start outlining your model with black paint; follow the lines of the face, hair, and clothing. You can pretend you are tracing a photograph; this may help you to find your "outlines."

4. If you make a mistake, it is very simple to correct it by wiping it away carefully with a slightly damp sponge. Then, dry the area with a paper towel and start again.

5. When you are done outlining, remember to thank your model. You can "paint in" your person when your black outlines are dry, but you do not need a model for this step.

6. At different times of the year, you may wish to add or subtract clothing (hat, gloves, coats, and so forth) according to the weather.

Jungle Resist

Jungle Resist

MATERIALS:

- newspaper
- crayons (all but purple, brown, and black)
- 12" x 18" heavy white paper
- pencil and eraser
- watered-down black tempera paint and brush

DIRECTIONS:

1. Study the jungle paintings of Henri Rousseau.

2. Draw your idea for a jungle on heavy, white paper. Include exotic, large-leaved plants, animals, and birds that are in trees as well as on the ground. Include textures in your leaves and in the skin coverings of animals and birds.

3. Trace over your pencil outlines with crayon, pressing hard on the crayon as you do this.

4. Begin to fill in outlined areas with various patterns and designs. Remember to use bright or fluorescent colors as these will show up best when your picture is painted.

5. Place your picture on top of newspaper and paint across the entire surface with watered-down black tempera.

6. The paint will "resist" your crayon lines and fill in any empty spaces in your picture.

Pointillism

Pointillism

MATERIALS:

- **9" x 12" drawing paper**
- **pencil and eraser**
- **oil pastels or Cray-Pas®**
- **slides or reproductions of paintings by Georges Seurat**

DIRECTIONS:

1. Pointillism was a style of painting popularized by a small group of French painters at the turn of the twentieth century. The most famous Pointillist painter was Georges Seurat, and it would be very helpful to look at examples of his work before starting this lesson.

2. When you look closely at a Pointillist painting, you will notice the use of tiny dots instead of areas of solid color. By using dots of color, the artist can create many interesting effects.

3. One effect you can experiment with is color mixing. Place tiny yellow dots right next to tiny blue dots, and then step back from your picture. Do you see a new color?

4. Next, place tiny red dots next to tiny blue dots and step back. What do you see? If yellow and blue dots appear to look green when you step back and blue and red dots appear to look purple, you are on the right track. If you do not see any change, perhaps it is because you made more blue dots than yellow ones or more red dots than blue. Keep experimenting to see what other combinations you can create.

5. After experimenting, choose a subject for your painting and lightly sketch it onto your white paper.

6. Then, starting with your lightest colors, begin to fill in your picture with tiny dots of color. You can do this by tapping your paper with the Cray-Pas®. Many dots close together will make a color look darker. This is good to know for creating shadows and outlines.

Sand Paintings

Sand Paintings

MATERIALS:

- **1 sheet of 12" x 18" black paper**
- **pencil**
- **watered-down white glue**
- **glue brush**
- **paper cup full of sand**
- **newspaper**

The Navajo Indians of America were probably the most famous at using **sand painting** as part of several important healing ceremonies. Their sand was ground from nearby cliffs, shells, charcoal, and pollen. Showing great skill, the artist reconstructed the designs from memory, dropping the colored sand with his thumb and forefinger. The designs showed many symbols for gods and spirits, the rainbow, mountains, animals, and plants. The Navajos, without a written language, kept their beliefs and legends alive with their sand painting.

DIRECTIONS:

1. Sketch your picture on the black paper. Try to keep your picture simple and large.

2. Spread newspaper under your black paper. Begin to paint over your outlines with the glue mixture. Only paint a small portion at a time (so that the glue will not dry before you can add the sand).

3. Next, sprinkle sand over the portion of the picture you have painted. Let it set for a minute, and then lift your paper and pour the excess sand back into the paper cup.

4. Sand paintings look best when you use lines and designs rather than solidly painted areas to fill your picture.

Warm and Cool Colors

Warm and Cool Colors

MATERIALS:

- **1 sheet of 12" x 18" white paper**
- **pencil and eraser**
- **ruler, tempera paints, and brushes**

Certain colors are thought of as warm and others as cool. We say this because certain colors—such as red, yellow, and orange—seem to make us feel warm, while other colors—like blue and green—seem to make us feel cool. Most of the time, artists use a combination of **warm and cool colors** in their paintings, but sometimes to create a powerful effect they may decide to create a painting using only warm colors or only cool colors.

DIRECTIONS:

1. In this activity, you will be able to observe this "effect" firsthand. You will be creating either a warm picture or a cool one.

2. Begin by drawing a picture on the white paper. If you are going to use warm colors, then draw a warm picture—for example, a hot summer day, a race car, or a forest fire blazing.

3. If you are going to use cool colors, then draw a cool picture—for example, an underwater scene, a snowball fight, or perhaps Eskimos ice fishing.

Monochromatic Painting

Monochromatic Painting

MATERIALS:

- 12" x 18" manila paper
- 12" x 18" heavy white paper
- pencil and eraser
- 4 baby food jars
- craft sticks
- tempera paint
- masking tape
- brushes

Monochromatic means a color scheme using shades and tints of only one color.

DIRECTIONS:

1. Draw a sketch of a landscape for your painting. It could be underwater, in outer space, or anywhere that you want it to be.

2. Copy it onto your white paper. An easy way to copy is to tape your first drawing under the white paper, tape this to a window, and trace the drawing.

3. A monochromatic painting uses dark and light shades or values of only one color.

4. Begin preparing your paints by filling two baby food jars each about one-third of the way with the one basic color you have chosen. To one jar, add nothing; to the other jar add a small amount of black paint.

5. Begin your third-color jar by filling it about one-third of the way with white paint. To this jar add a very small amount of your chosen color.

6. Make your fourth-color jar by filling it about one-third of the way with black paint. To this jar, add a small amount of your chosen color.

7. Mix each color with a craft stick. You should now have four very different shades or values of the color you have chosen.

8. You can now see that adding white always lightens a color and that adding black always darkens a color.

9. Using the correct size brush for each area, begin to paint in the landscape.

10. Try to use high contrast colors (colors that are light next to colors that are dark) to make the objects and shapes stand out clearly.

11. If you run into the problem of an object or shape not showing up, you can outline that shape with a darker or lighter color.

12. Remember never to paint next to a "wet" area. Paint in another part of the paper and come back to that area when it is dry.

13. When working this small, it is best to hold your hand as far down the brush next to the bristles as you can because you will have better control.

Multimedia Slides

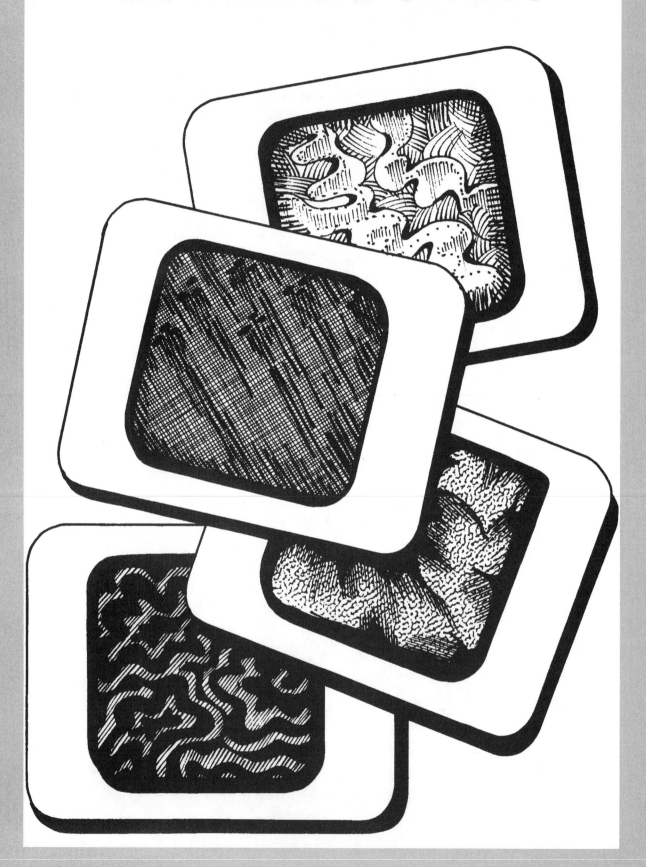

Multimedia Slides

MATERIALS:

- slide projector
- 2" x 2" cardboard or plastic slide mounts
- treated plastic acetate cut into 4" x 6" squares
- 2" acetate squares to cover and protect slides
- paper cups and craft sticks for mixing

- iron (used with adult supervision)
- various solutions such as spray paints, hair spray, bleach, dyes, inks, and so forth
- eyedroppers
- tissue paper, onion skins, hair, open-weave material, leaves, insect wings, and so forth

DIRECTIONS:

1. Use the materials on the 4" x 6" acetate squares and develop slides by mixing and dropping solutions into liquids already on the acetate. Let dry.

2. Prepare a slide for each below:
   a. shape
   b. line
   c. color
   d. texture
   e. space
   f. light (transparent, translucent, opaque)

3. Examine the results, then select and cut out the most interesting 2" square you can find in each of the larger pieces.

4. You may place additional "sheer" materials mentioned above on the acetate and then place a second piece of clear acetate on the painted surface of the slide to be mounted.

5. When ready to mount, make sure it fits into the inner frame of the slide mount. Then, fold the top of the slide mount over the two pieces of acetate and press the *sides* of the mount with a hot iron. This will cause the waxed edges of the mount to seal.

6. At another time, try gathering other materials brought in from home.

7. Images can be projected onto canvas for paintings.

Section III
Color and Design

LEVEL 4

Art Object Designs takes a commonplace object and uses it as a design element and to reinforce the techniques of collage and overlapping. Visual, rather than tactile, texture is given concentration in *Magazine Textures* as is the study of the composition of the whole from parts. The technique of "mosaic" is introduced in *Paper Mosaic* and in *Geometric Pictures.* In these lessons, paper cut in geometric shapes is used to form a composition. The project *Rainbow Pictures* reinforces the use of paper and includes the use of the contrast of patterned paper and solid colors.

Paper Mosaic

LEVEL 5

Advanced use of assorted materials is used in *Multimedia Mosaic,* which offers additional work in this art technique. Negative and positive areas are introduced in *Negative/Positive Designs* and are shown as an integral part of all artwork. Surface design is further studied in *Design a Van* as is further compositional exploration within a specified shape. *Candy Jars* provides continual compositional exploration including overlapping and objects placed on top of one another. In *One Line Only* creative problem solving using only one type of line alternating the length and width is explored.

Design a Van

LEVEL 6

Color and Design involves a paper and color design project emphasizing shape and the use of repetition, and it is also an informal introduction to positive and negative design. *Radial Designs* emphasizes and reinforces pattern and repetition and introduces the radiating technique of creating a design. The concept of illusion in art design is explored in *Optical Illusions,* where precise graphic art is presented. *Lettering* introduces the art of calligraphy.

Lettering

Art Object Designs

Art Object Designs

MATERIALS:

- 1 sheet of 12" x 18" white paper
- pencils and kneaded eraser
- art equipment: rulers, tape, protractors, scissors, compass, paper clips
- thick black marker
- colored markers or tempera paints and brushes

DIRECTIONS:

1. Soften your kneaded eraser in the warmth of your hand and then remove a small piece of it and use it to secure an art object to your paper. This object might be any of the things that are listed above. With your object anchored in place, take a pencil and trace around it.

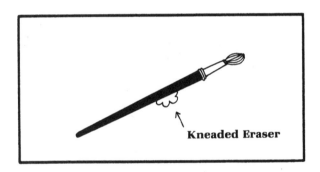

Kneaded Eraser

2. Continue to trace other objects, overlapping the objects but still doing complete outlines.

3. When your composition is complete, use your black marker to go over your pencil outlines. Remember to do complete outlines even when objects overlap.

4. After your black outlines are finished, you can begin to color in with markers (or tempera paints) the new shapes created by your overlapping outlines.

5. At this point, the objects themselves become less important and your new design emerges.

Magazine Textures

Magazine Textures

MATERIALS:

- 9" x 12" oaktag
- magazines
- scissors and glue
- pencil and eraser

Texture is the surface of anything, from rough to smooth. It may be a real surface or a visual impression of a texture, such as an actual mountain range or a picture of one in a magazine.

DIRECTIONS:

1. Cut out textural sections of magazine ads or illustrations until you have a good selection of colors and types.

2. Draw a simple landscape on the oaktag.

3. Cut sections with appropriate colors and textures to fit each object and glue them in.

4. Try to use light colors next to dark colors for contrast.

237

Paper Mosaic

Paper Mosaic

MATERIALS:

- **gummed paper tapes in a variety of colors**
- **12" x 18" black paper**
- **pencil and eraser**
- **12" x 18" manila paper**
- **egg carton**
- **glue**
- **scissors**
- **variety of metallic papers and colored magazine ads**
- **slides or photos of mosaics (see below)**

A **mosaic** is a picture or decoration made by joining together minute pieces of glass, stone, tile, wood, or other substances of different colors.

DIRECTIONS:

1. Study slides or photos of Greek, Roman, or Far Eastern mosaics.

2. Draw a single idea for your mosaic on the manila paper.

3. Next, place your manila paper drawing on top of the black paper, and then use a pencil to retrace all the lines in your picture. Press very hard on the pencil while doing this so that a clear impression of your picture will be made on the black paper.

4. Now, decide which colors of paper tape you will need for your picture, and then cut them up into tiny pieces. You may wish to use an egg carton to separate and save your multicolored pieces of paper tape.

5. Next, begin to fill in the various parts of your picture with the tiny pieces of colored tape. Place the shapes close together but not touching, as shown in the following example.

6. Try to place light colors next to dark colors for high contrast. This will make the objects show up more.

7. For interest, you might also want to use metallic paper or portions of the colored ads from magazines.

Geometric Pictures

Geometric Pictures

MATERIALS:

- **1 sheet of white 12" x 18" paper**
- **scissors**
- **white glue**
- **assorted colors of construction paper**
- **pencil**

DIRECTIONS:

1. Begin by cutting up a variety of colored paper into an assortment of geometric shapes of all sizes, such as fat and skinny triangles, long and short rectangles, big and small circles, and so forth.

2. Now, begin to arrange these in different ways on your white paper. What can you combine your shapes to create? You may wish to overlap some shapes and also cut some new shapes to fit a particular idea.

3. Plan your finished picture and very lightly make pencil outlines to help you place your shapes in the right place. See if you can make a very detailed picture. You can create designs and patterns by repeating the same shape over and over again or by alternating a few different shapes repeatedly.

Rainbow Pictures

Rainbow Pictures

MATERIALS:

- **white glue**
- **multicolor strips of varying widths**
- **2 sheets of black construction paper**
- **pencil and scissors**

Collage is a French word that means gluing or pasting. As an art term it means to assemble, arrange, and paste materials to create an artistic composition.

DIRECTIONS:

1. Using white glue, cover one sheet of black paper with a series of brightly colored paper strips of varying widths.

2. When dry, turn this sheet over and outline the things you wish to cut out to create your picture.

3. Next, place your cutouts on black construction paper and combine the lines and patterns to create interesting effects.

Multimedia Mosaic

Multimedia Mosaic

MATERIALS:

- **seeds, beans, macaroni**
- **glue**
- **12" x 18" heavy cardboard**
- **12" x 18" manila paper**
- **pencil and eraser**
- **carbon paper**

DIRECTIONS:

1. Draw a simple idea for your mosaic.

2. Use carbon paper to transfer it to cardboard.

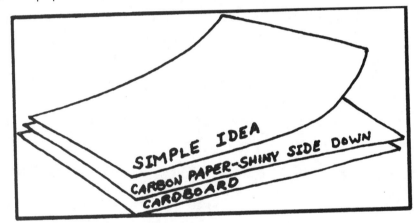

3. Divide your picture into areas and begin to glue different mosaic pieces into each. Be careful to place light-colored pieces next to dark-colored pieces to enable various objects to show up by this contrast.

4. All areas of the cardboard should be covered, so place the pieces close together.

Negative/Positive
Designs

Negative/Positive Designs

MATERIALS:

- **9" x 12" white drawing paper**
- **white glue**
- **4" x 6" black construction paper**
- **pencil**
- **scissors**

DIRECTIONS:

1. Center your 4" x 6" sheet of black paper on top of your 9" x 12" sheet of white paper and lightly trace around your black sheet. This outline will help you line up with your shapes later on.

2. Now, begin to draw and cut out shapes around all four sides of your black sheet. Place the shapes to the right of your pencil lines and keep them in order as you cut them out.

Pencil Outline

3. When all your shapes are cut out, glue down the large sheet first and then glue the shapes in their correct "reversed" place.

Design a Van

Design a Van

MATERIALS:

- **12" x 18" paper**
- **pencil and eraser**
- **colored markers**
- **thin black marker**

DIRECTIONS:

1. Draw the side of a van on 12" x 18" paper.

2. Draw a scene or design you would like to paint on the side of your van.

3. Outline all pencil lines with a thin, black marker and fill in the areas with colored markers.

Candy Jars

Candy Jars

MATERIALS:

- 12" x 18" paper
- pencil and eraser
- thin markers

DIRECTIONS:

1. Draw a large glass jar with a lid big enough so that you fill the entire paper vertically.

2. Inside the jar, draw in as many different types of candy as you can remember.

3. Draw each candy in detail and make all the candy appear piled on top of each other by overlapping the pieces and showing them at different angles.

4. Use the markers to color in the jar and candy.

One Line Only

One Line Only

MATERIALS:

- pencil and eraser
- 1 sheet of white 9" x 12" paper
- assorted thick markers and thin markers

DIRECTIONS:

1. This is a lesson in creative problem solving. Your goal is to create a picture using only one type of line—a straight one.

2. Begin by lightly sketching your idea in pencil on the white paper.

3. Next, begin to fill in your picture with lines. You will have to alternate the length, the width, and the direction of your lines in order to make your drawing visible.

Thick and Thin

Close Together and Far Apart

Alternating Direction

Creating Curves

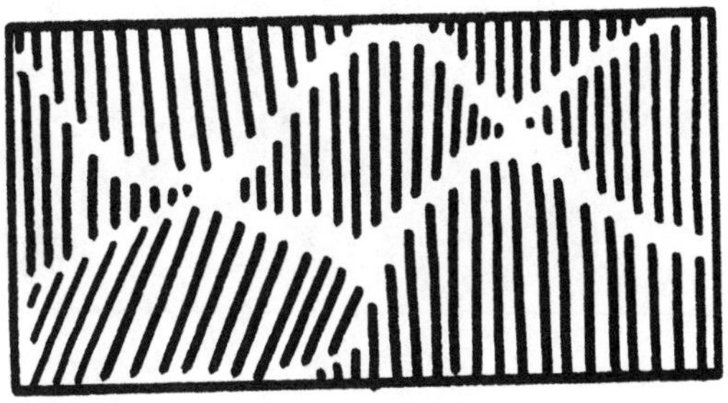

Color and Design

Color and Design

MATERIALS:

- 18" x 24" construction paper
- pencils and erasers
- sharp scissors
- paste or glue

- sixteen 4 ½" x 6" rectangles of construction paper (4 each of 4 colors)

DIRECTIONS:

1. In order to create 16 rectangles, fold a sheet of 18" x 24" construction paper in half four times.

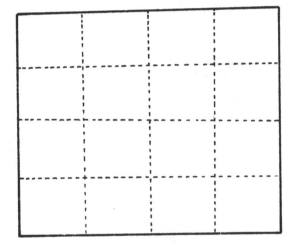

2. Next, choose four colors and cut out 16 rectangles 4 ½" x 6" in size (four in each color).

3. Choose a shape for each color category. Shapes that touch the tops and sides of the rectangle seem to work best. See the following illustrations.

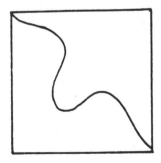 

4. Cut out three identical shapes in each category using your first shapes as patterns.

5. Place four different shapes in each row and continue to do this in each subsequent row.

Radial Designs

Radial Designs

MATERIALS:

- pencils
- crayons
- watered-down black tempera paint
- rulers
- manila or white paper
- brush

DIRECTIONS:

1. What do a dart board, a starfish, a Ferris wheel, and a flower have in common? For one thing, they are all good examples of radial designs. Radial designs are generated outward from a center point creating a circular pattern or design.

2. Find the center of your paper and mark it with a pencil dot.

3. Next, use your ruler to draw (*very lightly*) one line from your dot to the center top of the paper and another line to the center bottom. Then, make a line that goes from your center dot to the edge of each side of your paper. Next, draw a line from the top left side of your paper to the bottom right and another one from the top right to the bottom left side of your paper. These lines will serve as guidelines as you build up your design.

4. Starting at your center dot, begin to create shapes that will radiate toward the edges of your paper. For example, suppose you choose a triangle as your first shape. To make it radiate from the center, you would also make an identical triangle opposite your first one and then a triangle on each side. Notice that your design has changed to a square when it is complete.

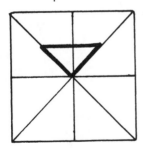 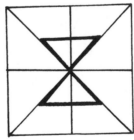 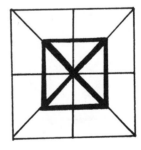

5. Continue to build up your design one shape at a time. You will be surprised at how many times it changes.

6. When you are done with your design, go over it in crayon. Press very hard and try to avoid using dark colors. You can make new patterns with color now by filling in some shapes with dots and others with stripes or wavy lines.

7. When you are done, brush the tempera over your design, painting evenly in rows and being careful not to repaint any areas.

Optical Illusions

Optical Illusions

MATERIALS:

- pencil and eraser
- 9" x 12" white paper
- thin black markers
- medium black markers
- ruler and compass

DIRECTIONS:

1. Measure your paper into ½" sections and draw vertical lines across the paper.

2. Inside, draw one large geometric shape. Next, repeat the shape inside or next to the first in varying sizes until the space seems filled, as shown.

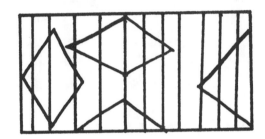

3. Begin with the top of the vertical space on your left and moving down, label lightly with a pencil each space you meet, alternately beginning with *B* for black and then *W* for white as shown. Continue until all spaces are marked by a *B* or a *W*. Alternate the labeling with each row or space.

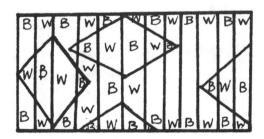

4. When all spaces are labeled, begin to carefully color them in using the black markers in the areas labeled *B*.

5. When you are finished, erase all the *W*s.

Lettering

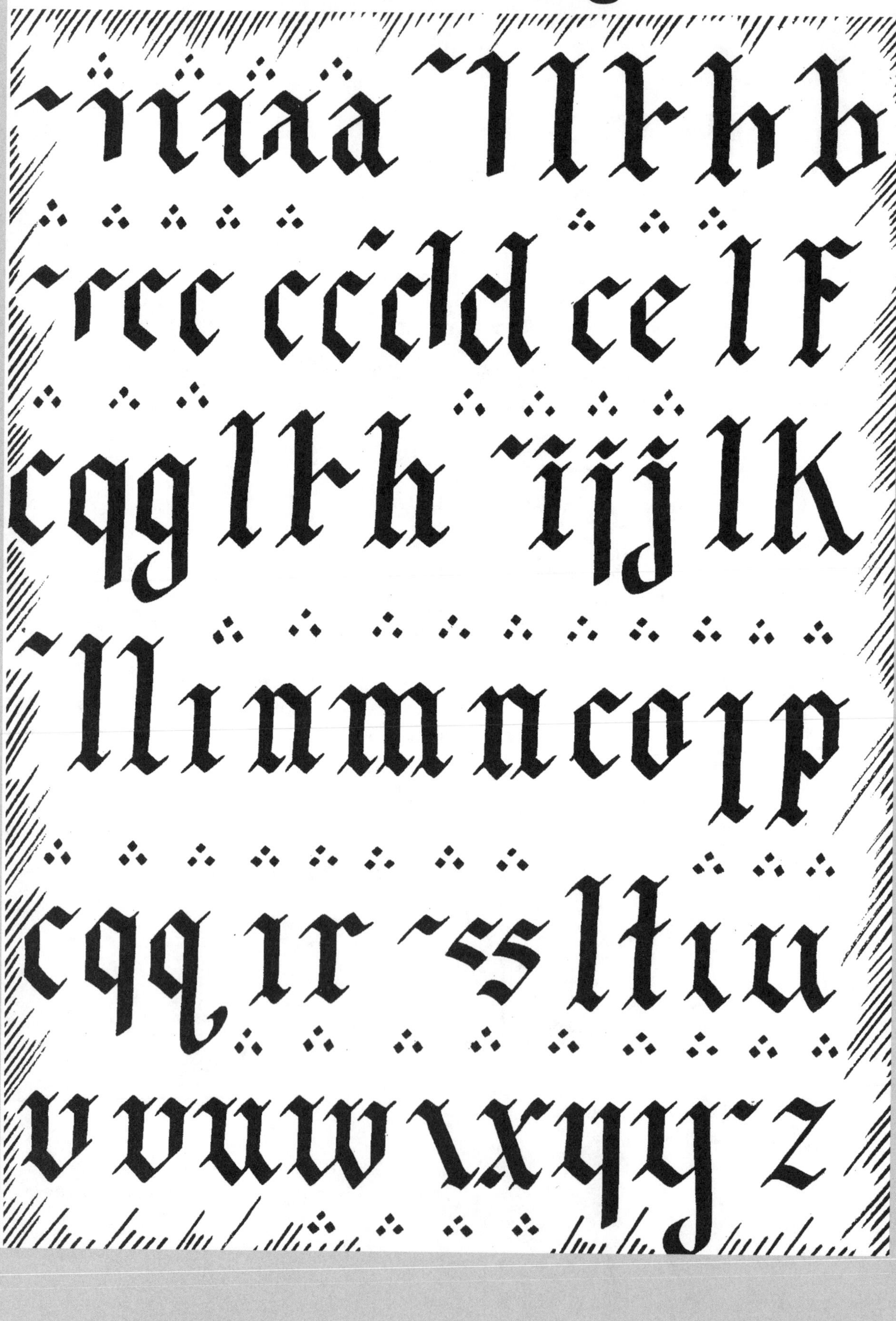

‾ ˙ı ˙ıï˙ıïäa ˘ lllkhb

‾rcc ccdcd ce lF

cqglth ˙˙ïïj lK

‾llinmncoıp

cqq ır ˘s lItiu

v v u u w ıxxyy ‾z

Lettering

MATERIALS:

- **chisel-point markers**
- **graph paper**
- **practice paper**

DIRECTIONS:

1. The letters you see in the illustration can all be created by using combinations of a few simple strokes.

2. First, familiarize yourself with the pen, noting that a chisel point or calligraphy marker has a tip shaped like this. This enables it to make thick as well as thin lines. Try making both on a piece of practice paper.

3. Using graph paper, you are ready to learn your first stroke, which is a thick vertical line. Try to make these very straight.

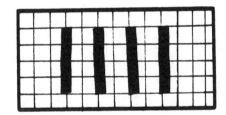

4. The next stroke consists of two thin diagonal lines connected by one thick one.

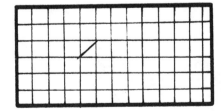 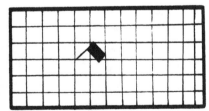

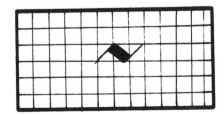

Practice these until they are easy to do. Try making some longer than others. See the following example.

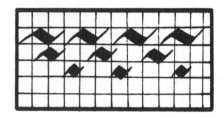

5. By combining the two strokes already learned, you can create a shape repeated very often in this alphabet. The shape is a letter *C*.

Stroke 2
Stroke 1
Stroke 2

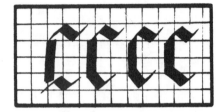

6. By looking at the alphabet in the illustration, see if you can find the *C* in the following letters.

7. When practicing your alphabet, always break the letter down into the strokes you recognize before starting. See the following examples.

Ceramics

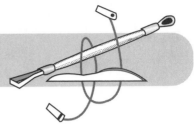

LEVEL 4

The concept of a mobile in clay is introduced in *Clay Mobiles* and the slab technique is reinforced. In *Treasure Boxes,* appliqué is given further emphasis as is advanced work in using the slab to create a box.

LEVEL 5

The concept of hollowing out is advanced in animal construction in *Clay Dinosaurs,* while continued work with slab and architectural elements is explored in *Clay Houses.*

LEVEL 6

Advanced study in animal observation and construction is carried forth in *Clay Animals.* In *Dream Car,* a further exercise using the slab is explored as is incised surface design. *Clay People* presents the clay construction of a human form incorporating all the elements presented in drawing the figure.

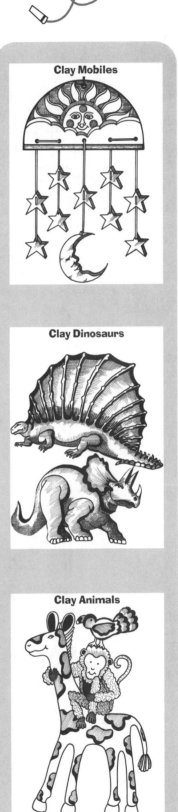

Clay Mobiles

Clay Dinosaurs

Clay Animals

Clay Mobiles

Clay Mobiles

MATERIALS:

- clay
- rolling pin
- newspaper
- pencil or dull knief
- cookie cutters (optional)
- manila paper
- nylon fishing twine or string
- tempera paints and brushes

A **mobile** is a hanging or standing construction or sculpture made of delicately balanced, movable parts.

DIRECTIONS:

1. On a piece of manila paper, plan your mobile and sketch it. Try to make your top piece and hanging pieces relate either through shape or idea. The example shows the daylight on top and the evening hanging in small pieces (the moon and stars).

2. When your sketch is complete, cut out your top piece and make a pattern of your smaller pieces. Place these on top of clay that you have rolled out to be about ¼" thick.

3. Cut out your clay shapes by either outlining them with a pencil or tracing around your paper shape with a dull knife.

4. On your top piece, make one hole in the center of the top with a pencil. Then make five or six holes about ½" from the bottom of your top piece. See the illustration.

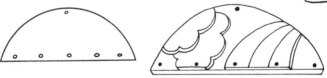

5. Next, decorate this piece by drawing shapes on it with a pencil or other clay tool, or build up the surface by adding clay shapes to it.

6. These can be put aside to be dried and later fired. When this process has been completed, they can be painted.

7. Cut out your small shapes with a paper pattern in the same way you cut out your top piece. You may also substitute cookie cutters if they will give you an appropriate shape. Make a small pencil hole in the top and bottom of each piece. The number of pieces you make will vary according to how full you want your mobile to look. Make a few extra shapes in case any break during the drying or firing process.

8. When all of your shapes have been fired and painted, use string or fishing twine to attach them to your top piece.

Treasure Boxes

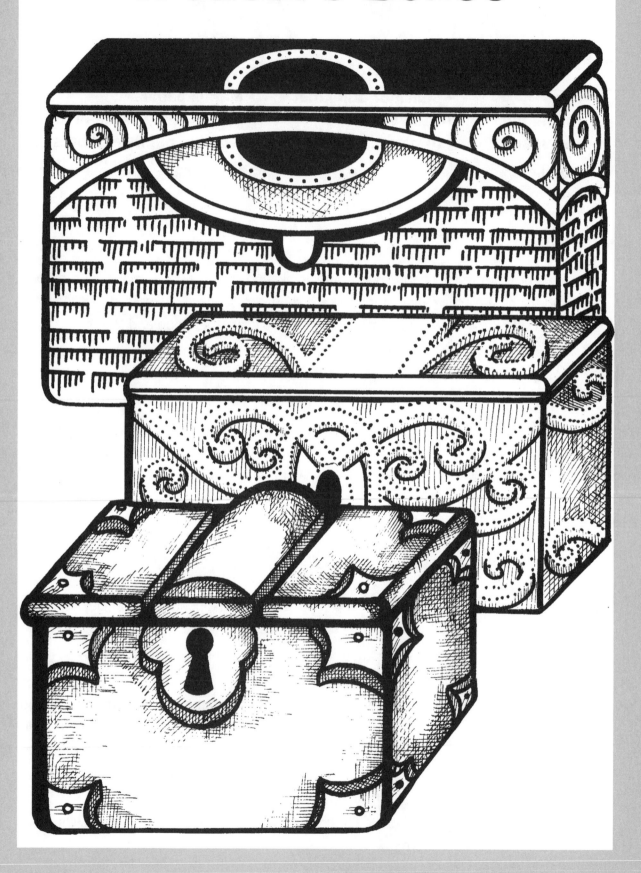

Treasure Boxes

MATERIALS:

- cardboard
- ruler, pencil, eraser, and scissors
- clay or kiln-firing or self-hardening clay
- two 10" lattice strips
- rolling pin
- modeling tools
- mat
- glaze
- cloth
- slip (water mixed with clay to the consistency of heavy cream, which is used to join clay pieces)
- paste brush

DIRECTIONS:

1. Using the cardboard, measure and draw some rectangles or squares as templates for the bottom and sides of your box.

2. On the mat, roll out a ball of clay between two lattice strips to ensure a uniformly thick slab.

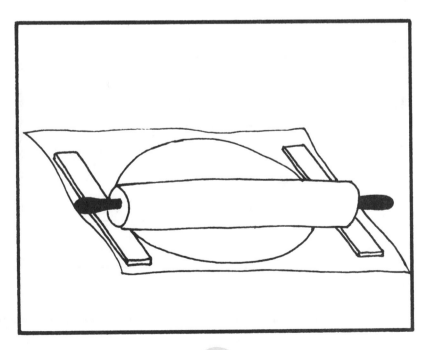

3. Lay the cardboard shapes on the slab and, using a thin modeling tool, cut around the cardboard and remove the excess clay.

4. Score the edges of the bottom of your box with a modeling tool and place some slip along the edge with a paste brush or with your finger.

5. Set your first wall on one of these edges; score both ends of this side slab and add some slip.

6. Continue doing the same with the other sides of your box. Join the corners using scoring and slip and, in addition, weld the clay together using your fingers or a modeling tool.

7. Inside each corner, place vertically a very thin coil and weld or blend one into each side to provide strength.

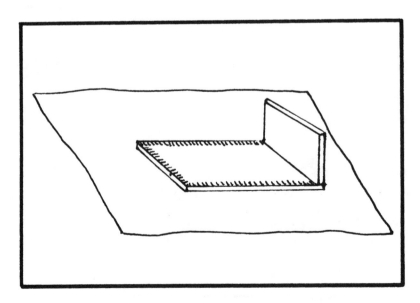

8. Coils may be added between the slabs to make a more interesting box, and they may also be used as a top edging or as a decoration on the box.

9. Try to make your box interesting enough to tempt someone to want to open it to discover its contents.

10. Measure the top for a lid and cut out a cardboard template.

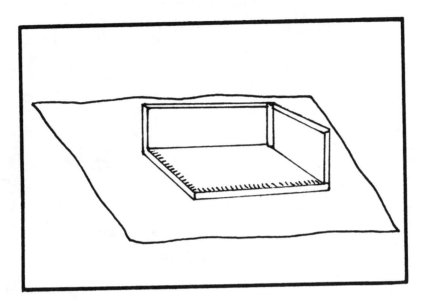

11. Roll out and cut a slab for the top and let this dry separately from the box.

12. Again, coils may be added to the top for interest.

13. Handles may be incorporated.

14. Let your box dry slowly with a damp cloth.

15. Fire and glaze.

Clay Dinosaurs

Clay Dinosaurs

MATERIALS:

- kiln clay or self-hardening clay
- modeling tools
- newspaper
- mats
- 12" x 18" paper
- pencil and eraser
- spoon

DIRECTIONS:

1. After research, draw a contour drawing of the dinosaur you want to model.

2. Observe the shape of the body and start by modeling this.

3. Hollowing out forms is necessary when clay is to be fired in a kiln.

4. Hollow out the inside with a spoon or a wire-looped modeling tool until the walls are about the thickness of your little finger.

5. Wad newspaper up tightly and stuff it inside the body of your dinosaur until it is completely filled.

6. Next, observe the legs. Are the shapes of the front legs the same as the back? Repeat the steps above for hollowing. Attach the legs by placing them where you want them and by adding more clay to make the joint strong. Finish by using your fingers to smooth out the surface of the joint.

7. Follow the steps above with the head, neck, and tail.

8. Use your tools to add any texture you desire to the skin.

9. Let dry slowly with a damp cloth draped over the form.

10. Fire and glaze.

Clay Houses

Clay Houses

MATERIALS:

- 9" x 12" paper
- photo of the front of your house
- pencil and eraser
- kiln-firing clay
- mat
- modeling tools
- ¼" x 1' wood slats
- rolling pin
- scissors

DIRECTIONS:

1. Draw a simple contour of the front of your house using the photograph. Cut out the drawing of your house.

2. Roll out clay between the slats so that you have a slab as large as your cutout drawing.

3. Using a thin modeling tool, cut around your drawing like a giant cookie.

4. Using a pencil, add lines for windows, doors, and so forth as they appear in your photograph.

5. Roll out additional slabs and cut out some of these parts to add in clay-appliqué technique, which will give your house a relief effect.

6. Using a tool in a twirling motion, make two holes at the top of your clay house about ½" from the edge so that you can hang your model.

7. Let it dry slowly under a damp cloth.

8. When leather-hard, brush off any excess bits of clay.

9. Let dry completely.

10. Fire and glaze.

Clay Animals

Clay Animals

MATERIALS:

- clay
- modeling clay tool
- wire-looped clay tool
- mat
- newspaper
- pencil and eraser
- paper

DIRECTIONS:

1. Draw a picture of the animal you wish to make. Pay attention to the details here so that you can use your drawing as a reference later while working on the clay.

2. Study your drawing and begin forming the body shape—usually an egg shape.

3. Add the legs next and decide whether you plan to make a reclining, sitting, or standing animal. Part of this will depend on whether the thickness of your animal's legs is sufficient to support the weight of its body when standing.

4. Clay parts must be added carefully and joined by smoothing the two parts together. You may even add a little additional clay when necessary for extra strength.

5. Scoop out the body with a wire-looped clay tool until no part of the body is thicker than your thumb.

6. If necessary, fill with crunched-up newspaper. This will support the body while you are working on it and will burn up in the kiln. Consequently, you do not have to remove the newspaper before you fire your clay model.

7. Next, add the neck and head, hollowing them out if they are thicker than your thumb and adding a hole in the body connecting with the hollow of the neck to let the air escape during firing as shown. If the legs are thicker than your thumb, they must also be hollowed out.

8. Add any details, smooth the clay so no cracks remain, and add skin textures or other features with modeling tools.

Dream Car

Dream Car

MATERIALS:

- clay
- slip
- modeling tools
- mat
- rolling pin
- ¼" x 1' wooden slats
- 9" x 12" oaktag
- scissors
- ceramic glazes
- acrylic paint
- brushes
- pencil

Relief is the projection of a part from the surface in sculpture or similar work.

DIRECTIONS:

1. Draw a picture of your dream car on the oaktag.

2. Cut out the pattern, roll out a clay slab between the wooden slats, lay your pattern on the slab, and cut it out carefully. Remove the excess clay.

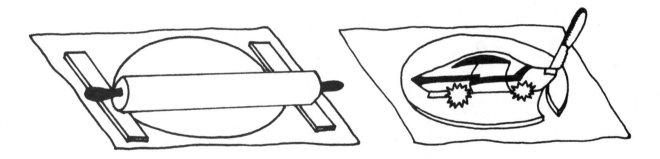

3. Using a pencil, draw in details from your drawing such as doors, headlights, windows, decorations, tires, and so forth.

4. Using other clay slabs, cut out some of these parts and attach them to your clay slab car using some slip and a modeling tool to join.

5. Let dry, fire, and glaze, or paint. If desired, fire again.

Clay People

Clay People

MATERIALS:

- **clay**
- **mat**
- **modeling tools**
- **glaze or paint and acrylic polymer**

DIRECTIONS:

1. Start with a piece of clay a bit larger than a ¼-pound stick of butter.

2. The entire figure, with the exception of the arms, should be shaped from the single piece of clay.

3. "Slice" one end of the clay so that two segments can be shaped to form the legs and feet.

4. The other end should be pinched and molded to form the neck and head.

5. Roll out two coils of clay for the arms and then attach them to the torso.

6. Once the basic shape is formed and the proportions established, positioning of the figure should be determined.

7. Avoid stiff, rigid positions in favor of those that are more natural and relaxed.

8. Position yourself in a pose you want your clay person to take and study how the arms and legs are bent. Get into the position yourself to get the idea.

9. Add details and finishing touches to give personality and expression to the figure.

10. Let dry, fire, and glaze, or paint and coat with acrylic polymer.

Paper Crafts

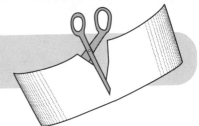

LEVEL 4

The project *Setting the Stage for Halloween* involves more advanced paper sculpture techniques within a confined space to create a stage setting, while *Halloween Mobiles* introduces the concept of a "mobile." *Three-Dimensional Silhouettes* provides further use with the silhouette as an art technique and more experience with precise paper cutting.

LEVEL 5

Cut Paper Masterpiece presents the concept of reducing a picture to its basic geometric shapes. *Paper Towers* examines repetition and pattern in cut paper designs to create a three-dimensional art form. The project *Kites* involves designing within an unconventional surface shape—a diamond—and provides further work with basic kite construction. *Colonial Pull Toys* introduces an historical use of art in toy construction, increased practice with characterization, and an understanding of body parts in action.

LEVEL 6

Flying Tetrahedrons explores a more advanced kite construction.

Three-Dimensional Silhouettes

Paper Towers

Flying Tetrahedrons

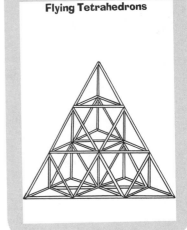

Setting the Stage
for Halloween

Setting the Stage for Halloween

MATERIALS:

- cardboard box
- construction paper
- variety of papers (metallic, fluorescent, and so forth)
- scissors
- glue, masking tape, clear tape

- thin wire
- cotton
- pipe cleaners
- craft sticks
- markers

DIRECTIONS:

1. Cut off the flaps on the box and cut down two corners as shown. The box should look like this.

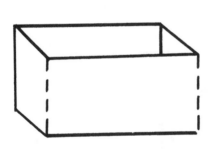 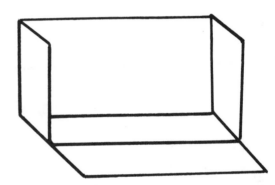

2. Glue paper on the inside and bottom of the box to simulate sky and ground.

3. If desired, glue paper to simulate hills in the background.

4. Imagine that you are designing a stage set for a play about Halloween. What would you want to include to create a scary atmosphere?

5. Review some basic paper sculpture techniques you might use:

Curling

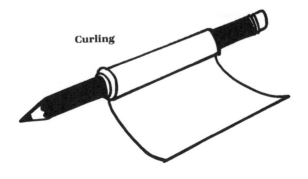

Fringing

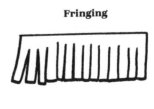

Tabs   **Cones**

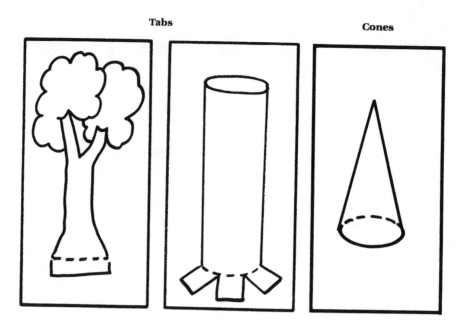

6. Begin by constructing a castle or a haunted house, as shown. Make it have three sides by folding and give it tabs so that it will stand. Cut out doors and windows. Draw shapes to simulate stone, brick, wood, and so forth on the outside walls before standing.

Glue

Glue

7. Glue the flaps and set up your construction.

8. Add other objects to create an eerie effect, such as ghosts, monsters, vampires, trees with scary objects in them, gravestones, and bridges over water filled with horrible creatures.

9. Use the thin wire to suspend flying witches, ghosts, bats, and so forth.

10. You may want to add a moon, dark clouds, or lightning to create the mood.

Halloween Mobiles

Halloween Mobiles

MATERIALS:

- manila paper
- 12" x 18" orange posterboard
- 9" x 12" black posterboard
- nylon fishing twine
- hole puncher

- markers
- scissors
- glue
- pencil

DIRECTIONS:

1. To begin, you'll need to make a large pumpkin shape on your orange posterboard. The best way to do this is to stand up, hold your pencil the way you would hold a piece of chalk, and move your arm in a circular motion right *above* your paper. When your imaginary circle is large enough to take up the whole paper, begin to let your pencil lightly touch the surface of the paper. Do this many times until you have a dark outline. See the following example.

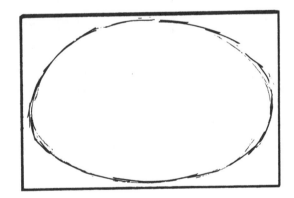

2. Cut along your outline and erase the extra lines. Next, sketch the lines that show the sections of the pumpkin's face. Afterward, go over these lines in black marker. Repeat this step on the other side also.

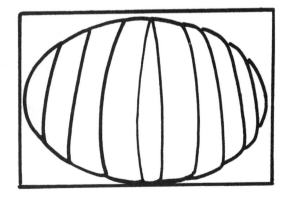

3. Next, sketch the line that will divide your pumpkin's face in half. It will also define your eyes, so draw it carefully. See the examples.

4. Afterward, cut along your lines. Then draw a mouth and nose on both the front and back of your pumpkin and color them in with a black marker.

5. Next, make a pattern for your bat eyes by folding a piece of manila paper in half and drawing a shape as shown from the fold.

6. Place your pattern on the black posterboard and trace and cut out two bats. Also, draw and cut out a stem and glue it to the top of your pumpkin.

7. Next, use a hole puncher to make holes in the following places.

8. Connect all the pieces with fishing twine and hang.

Three-Dimensional Silhouettes

Three-Dimensional Silhouettes

MATERIALS:

- 1 sheet of white 9" x 12" paper
- 1 sheet of black 9" x 6" paper
- pencil and eraser
- ruler
- scissors
- white glue
- crayons and markers

DIRECTIONS:

1. Holding your white paper horizontally, draw ½" margins along the right and left sides of your paper. Fold the paper toward the center along your pencil lines. Then use crayons or markers to create a scenic background for your silhouette.

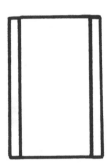 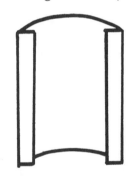 

2. Next, holding your black paper vertically, draw ½" margins along all four edges. Then, draw your silhouette making sure it is touching at least one of the four margins.

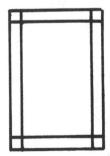 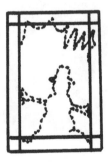

3. Now, cut away the areas surrounding your silhouettes. Then add glue to the left and right margins.

4. Attach the black paper to the white paper by lining up the glued margins with the folded white margins.

Cut Paper Masterpiece

Cut Paper Masterpiece

MATERIALS:

- reproduction of a famous painting
- 1 sheet of black 12" x 18"paper
- various sheets of colored paper
- pencil and eraser
- thin black marker
- tracing paper
- scissors
- glue

The illustration for this activity is based on the painting *Woman Pouring Milk* by **Jan Vermeer**. Vermeer lived and painted during the seventeenth century in Holland. Most of his paintings show us simple scenes of Dutch life. Vermeer is known as the "painter of light" because of the skillful and sensitive way he was able to capture the effects of light on the surfaces it altered.

DIRECTIONS:

1. You will be doing something very unusual in this lesson—something that you've always been told *not* to do. You will be tracing someone else's work. You will select a reproduction of a famous work and then place tracing paper on top of it and begin to outline the forms.

2. As you do this, shapes and forms you had hardly noticed will begin to emerge. Examine the different types of lines the artist has used. If you were drawing the picture, how would you have drawn the same thing?

3. The first illustration (Figure A) shows one small section of the large illustration in detail. It shows the left arm from the shoulder to the elbow. Compare this to Figure B, which shows the same area drawn simply. We can see that the artist has very carefully rendered every fold and crease in the fabric in Figure A after close observation and study. We notice that this attention to detail makes Figure A much more interesting to look at than Figure B.

Figure A **Figure B**

4. In Figure C, we see a tracing of just the head, which reveals all the small changes in light, shadow, and color. Your tracing does not have to be this detailed, but it does show you how complicated parts can be broken up.

Figure C

5. After you have finished outlining, begin to cut out your tracing, one piece at a time. As you do this, place it on a sheet of construction paper that is the appropriate color. Then trace it and cut it out.

6. Glue this shape onto your black construction paper. Continue to assemble your masterpiece in this way, almost like a puzzle.

Paper Towers

Paper Towers

MATERIALS:

- **assorted sheets of construction paper**
- **white glue or paste**
- **markers**
- **stapler**
- **scissors**
- **pipe cleaner**

DIRECTIONS:

1. **a.** Fold one sheet of construction paper in half lengthwise.

   b. Then fold it in half lengthwise again.

   c. When you open it up, flatten it out and cut along your three fold lines. This will give you four strips of paper that are the same length and width.

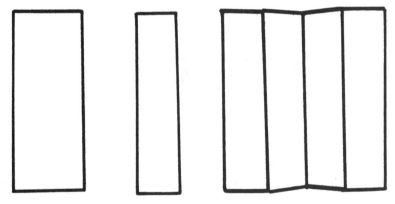

2. Now take two strips and overlap and glue them together to create one very long strip. Do the same thing to the two remaining strips.

3. Next cut out multicolored geometric shapes and glue them in a decorative pattern on the long strips.

4. When this is done, you are ready to attach thin paper strips to the bottom of your long strip. Try to space these evenly across a row.

5. When these are dry, you can attach your second long strip to the bottom with glue.

6. Continue to make row after row in the same manner. The more rows you make, the taller your tower will be. You can also experiment with strips of paper that connect the rows by using a criss-cross or diagonal pattern.

7. When all your rows are connected and dry, you can roll your tower into a cylinder shape by matching up the ends of the long strips and stapling them together.

8. To make a roof for your tower, cut out a black circle (about the size of a dinner plate), and then cut away a slice of it. Next, pull one edge of the circle under the other and staple them together as they overlap.

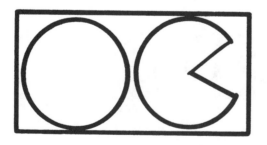 

9. Attach four wide strips to the base of this black top, and then staple the other ends of those four strips to the tower. Next, twist one end of a pipe cleaner into a knot and insert the other end through the point of the tower top. This will make it easy to hang your tower so that it can spin in the breeze.

Kites

Kites

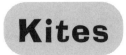

MATERIALS:

- 12" x 18" manila paper
- pencil and eraser
- tempera and brushes
- heavy butcher-grade paper
- scissors
- carpet twine or other strong thin string
- rulers
- 2 sticks (one 30" and one 36") of narrow lattice notched in the ends
- glue and masking tape

Kite making dates back to early Chinese history. Kites were used to deliver messages and used even in warfare. Today, kites are used for enjoyment and range in size, shape, and materials.

DIRECTIONS:

1. Draw a diamond shape for your kite on manila paper as shown.

2. Draw a design or picture inside this shape using all the space to compose your idea.

3. Lay the two sticks crossed with the shorter one horizontally across the longer one 7" down from the top (marked at the middle of 15"). Glue them together at this point and wrap a narrow piece of masking tape around them to hold them until they are dry. Make sure the sticks are not crooked.

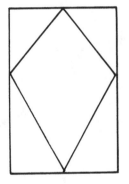

4. When the sticks are completely dry, run the string through one notched end and tie; pass it on to the next notched stick, keeping the string taut and then on to the next, and the next, and then back to the last stick and tie.

5. Lay the strung kite frame on heavy paper and trace the string kite shape, holding it firmly with your other hand while you trace.

6. Remove the frame and add a 1" border all the way around to allow for some paper to be folded and glued over the string frame.

7. Draw your design or picture on the large paper kite form and paint. Let dry.

8. Lay your painted kite design under your frame, backside up, and carefully fold 1" borders over the string and glue them down. Let dry.

9. Bridle the kite on the front side as shown. The two strings should be tied about 4" away from the surface of the kite.

10. Attach flying string to the point where the two strings are joined.

Colonial Pull Toys

Colonial Pull Toys

MATERIALS:

- manila paper
- pencils and eraser
- posterboard in assorted colors
- 1 plastic straw
- scissors
- tape
- yarn or string
- 4 brass fasteners
- hole puncher
- markers or crayons

DIRECTIONS:

1. Begin by sketching your character on manila paper. Keep your shapes simple. Arms and legs should be drawn straight.

2. Next, cut out your entire figure and then cut the arms and legs from the torso. Use these cutouts as patterns on the posterboard. Trace around them and cut them out.

3. Use the hole puncher to place holes as shown. Then overlap the holes and join the parts with brass fasteners.

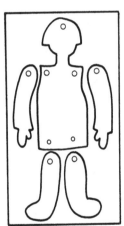 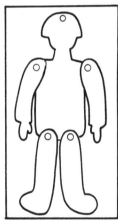

4. Now use markers or crayons to color in and decorate your character.

5. Next, cut four 1" lengths from the plastic straw. Attach one to the back of each arm and leg with tape as shown.

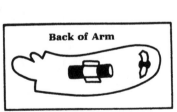

Back of Arm

6. Cut four 15" lengths of string or yarn. Tie a large knot at the end of each one and thread one through each straw as shown.

7. Gather all four strings into a knot and trim the strings to the same length.

8. Pull the strings and watch what happens.

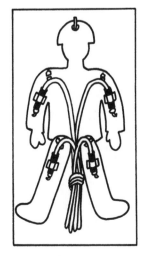

Flying Tetrahedrons

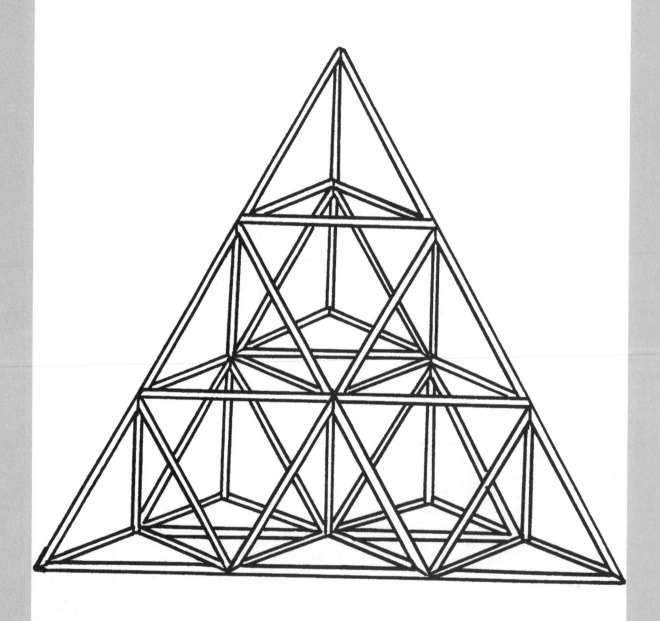

Flying Tetrahedrons

MATERIALS:

- white glue
- 60 paper straws
- brightly colored tissue paper
- scissors and string

A **tetrahedron** is a triangular pyramid.

DIRECTIONS:

1. To begin making your kite, start by carefully joining six straws together with glue as shown. Then cover two sides with tissue paper. This completes one unit. In order to make a kite you need ten units.

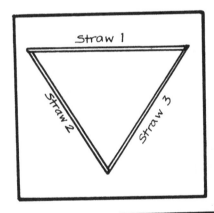 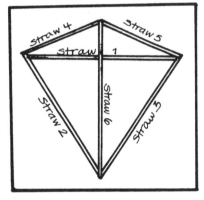

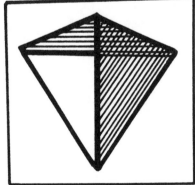

2. When you have completed ten units, assemble your kite with glue by aligning the corners of each unit and making sure they are all facing in the same direction.

3. Attach a string to each corner of your base and then join these three strings together in a knot. Add a long strip to this knot and go fly your kite.

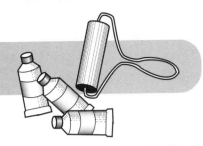

Section VI
Printmaking

LEVEL 4

Styrofoam Texture Prints explores printmaking further by using incised shapes to create various textures.

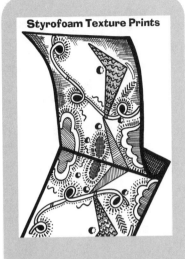

Styrofoam Texture Prints

LEVEL 5

Linoleum Block Prints introduces a new medium, linoleum, and reinforces the use of texture and pattern, as well as negative and positive areas in printmaking.

Linoleum Block Prints

LEVEL 6

Silk-Screen Prints illustrates a more advanced printmaking technique using a stencil, while *Glue Prints* explores the "line" quality of printmaking in a relief style.

Silk-Screen Prints

Styrofoam
Texture Prints

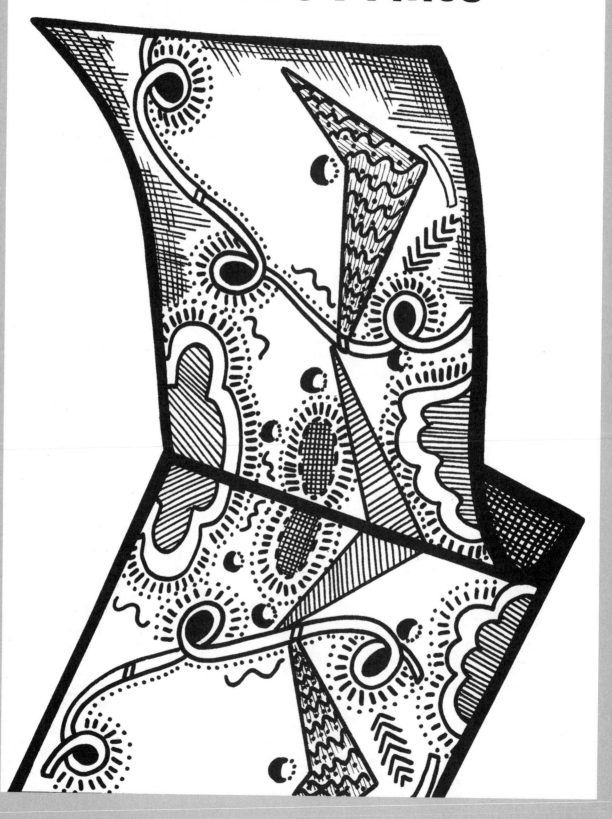

Styrofoam Texture Prints

MATERIALS:

- **Styrofoam meat trays**
- **hard textural objects such as keys, gears, screws, combs, shells, and so forth**
- **scissors**

- **water-based printing ink**
- **printing trays**
- **brayers**
- **printing paper**

First the Egyptians and then the Chinese and Japanese made hand-carved **relief designs** that could be reproduced in numbers. Later, blocks were carved to print textiles in Europe. Children begin life by making a print. A nurse applies some ink to the soles of a baby's feet and the doctor presses them against paper.

DIRECTIONS:

1. Cut off the edges of the Styrofoam tray so that you are left with a flat piece.

2. Using various textural objects, press a design deeply into the Styrofoam.

3. As with any composition, try to include some large, some medium, and some small designs.

4. Roll out ink and roll over the design.

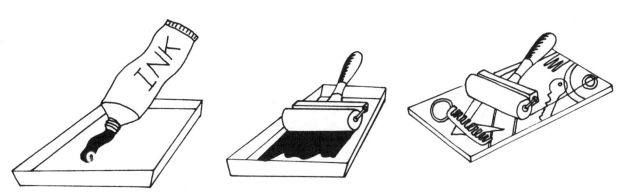

5. Lay printing paper on the design and rub the back of the paper with your fingertips.

6. Carefully peel off the print and let dry.

Linoleum Block Prints

Linoleum Block Prints

MATERIALS:

- 9" x 12" manila paper
- 9" x 12" unmounted linoleum block
- linoleum cutting tools
- pencil and eraser
- carbon paper
- thin black markers and thick black markers
- water-based printing ink
- inking tray
- brayer
- baren or wooden spoon
- safety metal bench hook
- absorbent printing paper
- masking tape

DIRECTIONS:

1. Draw your idea for the linoleum block on the manila paper. Add textural areas to make the drawing more interesting. Shade in certain areas completely. You should end up with one-third of the areas white, one-third of the areas dark, and one-third textured.

2. Lay carbon paper on your block shiny side down. Lay your drawing over this and attach it with masking tape; trace over the lines, pressing hard with a pencil to transfer the drawing to the block.

3. Trace over all lines, textures, and shaded areas with black markers.

4. Lay the bench hook over the edge of the table and the linoleum block on top.

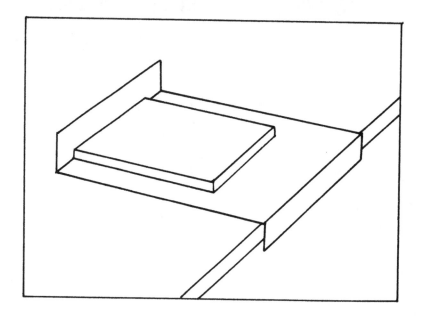

5. Pick up a #2 outlining cutter and hold it so that the handle end is inside your palm and your index finger is on top of the handle.

6. Lay your other hand across the bottom of the block as shown; rest the hand that holds the cutter on top of this hand for safety as shown.

7. Always slice toward the back of the bench hook so that if you slip, you will hit only this. Turn the block when necessary so that you always cut only in this direction.

8. Always keep the hand without the tool resting on the bottom of the block under your other hand for safety.

9. Cut out the outlines of all shapes.

10. Change cutters as necessary to cut out textures and solid areas.

11. Squeeze out ink on a tray and roll over it with a brayer until the tray is evenly covered with ink.

12. Roll ink onto the block quickly.

13. Lay absorbent paper on the block and rub the back of the block with a baren, with the back of a wooden spoon, or with your fingers.

14. Carefully peel off the paper and hang it to dry.

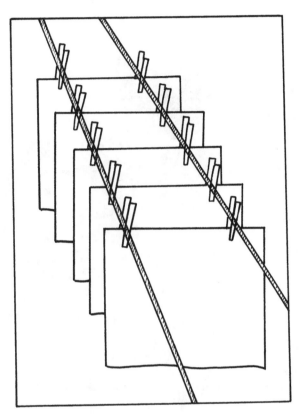

SIMPLE REDUCTION PRINT

This technique can be used to produce a multicolor print by cutting away only part of a block, printing it in one color, and letting it dry; then cutting away a little more, printing it in a second color, and letting it dry; and finally cutting away the remainder, printing it, and letting it dry.

Silk-Screen Prints

Silk-Screen Prints

MATERIALS:

- prepared silk screen
- water-based printing ink
- pencil and eraser
- 2 oaktag pieces the size of the inside of the wood frame
- construction paper
- squeegee
- craft knife
- tape

Silk screen is a stencil process using fine cloths that have been painted with an impermeable coating except in areas where color is to be forced through onto paper, cloth, and so forth.

DIRECTIONS:

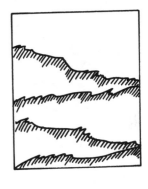

1. Draw different "line" shapes on one piece of oaktag to make a stencil. Lines may overlap, as shown.
2. Draw different shapes of varying sizes on the other piece of oaktag to make a stencil. Shapes may overlap.
3. Cut out the lines and shapes with the craft knife.
4. Select a piece of construction paper.
5. Select a color of ink that contrasts with the color of paper you chose.

6. Lift the screen and lay the piece of construction paper on the base piece of wood. Mark the corners of the paper with masking tape so that if you want to make additional prints, you can put each paper in the same position.
7. Next, lay the first stencil on the construction paper.
8. Lay the screen down on the paper and place blobs of ink along one edge of the screen.
9. Using the squeegee, push the ink from one end to the other and back again, forcing the ink through the screen and the holes in the oaktag. Push back and forth several times.
10. Lift the screen and remove the paper to dry.
11. Wash out the screen with running water and a mild liquid soap. Let dry completely. You may even set it in front of a fan.
12. When the first paper is dry, place it under the screen with the second stencil and repeat the printing process with a second color.
13. Let dry.

Glue Prints

Glue Prints

MATERIALS:

- white glue in a squeeze bottle
- 12" x 18" cardboard
- pencil and eraser
- 12" x 18" manila paper
- mimeograph paper or woodblock printing paper
- brayer and wooden spoon

DIRECTIONS:

1. Make a sketch of a simple idea for your print. Make sure your idea fills the space and has one large item that is the most important object in the print.

2. Transfer the drawing to the cardboard.

3. Leave the cap off the container of glue overnight so that it will thicken to a manageable texture.

4. Squeeze the glue along the pencil lines. When dry, you may need a second application along the same lines of the glue to "stand up" high enough in relief to make a print.

5. Set the design aside to dry. It may take several days for the glue to dry completely and to be hard enough to be used for inking and printing.

6. The plate is inked in the same manner as a linoleum cut. An ink-loaded brayer is rolled over the surfaces of the plate and the raised glue lines receive the ink. Some ink will also be retained by background sections. This will produce interesting textured areas in contrast to the more highly defined glue lines.

7. The print is made by carefully placing a sheet of paper over the plate and pressing down lightly on it.

8. Care should be taken so as not to move the paper and thereby blur the print.

9. Mimeograph paper is excellent for printing, but if woodblock printing paper is available, the results will be even finer.

10. Rubbing in a rotating motion with a wooden spoon or flat-surfaced object will produce an interesting print.

11. Many prints can be made from one plate, and the plate itself can be preserved and mounted.

Weaving

LEVEL 4

Op-Art Weaving expands on previous paper weaving using an uneven weft line to create a design, while *People Weavings* introduces a technique for creating a recognizable form within the weaving.

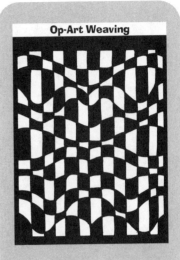

Op-Art Weaving

LEVEL 5

Textural Weaving explores more advanced weaving techniques such as the rya knot and fringe and the use of positive and negative space in weaving as well as the creation of different weaving patterns.

Textural Weaving

LEVEL 6

Basket Weaving involves weaving a three-dimensional object using reeds as a new media.

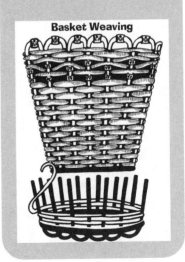

Basket Weaving

Op-Art Weaving

Op-Art Weaving

MATERIALS:

- **12" x 18" black paper**
- **12" x 18" white paper**
- **pencil and eraser**
- **scissors**
- **ruler**
- **glue**

During the 1960s, art became concerned with creating a tremendous impact on the eye. Intense, fluorescent color, or black and white together with sharply painted lines and shapes in extra large paintings excited the viewer. **Op-Art** or "Optical Art" was fun! Illusion was often the goal of the painter.

DIRECTIONS:

1. On the white paper, draw some smooth, curving lines the length of the paper as shown. Cut carefully and smoothly along the lines, and be sure to stop 1" from each edge.

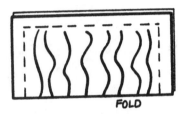

2. Lay the ruler on the end of the black paper the short way and draw a pencil line along the edge. Repeat from left to right across the paper as shown. Cut the strips.

3. Begin weaving the black strips through the white curving lines. Start on the left and weave *over* and *under* across the paper.

4. Alternate the next black strip through the white by going *under* and *over* across the paper.

5. Continue to alternate weaving the black strips completely across the paper until no more strips will fit in, as shown.

6. Glue all the ends of the black strips to the white paper and let dry.

People Weavings

People Weavings

MATERIALS:

- **looms (wood)**
- **yarn**
- **yarn needles**
- **12" x 18" paper**
- **pencil and eraser**

In every area of the world, **weaving** has been used. The materials that were used—such as grasses and reeds, wool, and animal pelts—were as varied as the climate. Clothing, shelters, baskets, blankets, and mats were made.

DIRECTIONS:

1. Draw a rectangle on paper the size of the loom.

2. Design simple hair, face, arms, skirts or pants, legs, feet, and shoes of a person you want to weave. Label the colors.

3. Remember that warp threads are the vertical threads and the weft threads run horizontally through the warp.

4. Insert the steel guideposts in each side of the loom to keep the weaving from angling inward. If your loom is handmade and does not come with steel guideposts, you may cut a piece of wire from a coat hanger and trim it to size.

5. Thread your loom by tying around the first notch, then pulling the yarn taut directly across to the notch on the other side, around this notch, and back. Continue until you reach the end and wrap your yarn around the last notch and knot.

6. Tie your first color yarn to the end warp and thread through a yarn needle. Continue to weave this color in and out in the areas for this color only.

7. When two colors meet, you must dovetail them so that both colors wrap around the same warp thread where they meet.

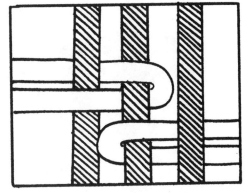

8. Continue working with your other colors until all areas are filled in. Remember to contrast light colors next to dark colors so that the different parts of the "person" show up.

Textural Weaving

Textural Weaving

MATERIALS:

- looms
- shuttles
- yarn needles
- yarn
- masking tape

DIRECTIONS:

1. Remember that warp threads are the vertical threads and the weft threads run horizontally, weaving through the warp.

2. Insert the steel guideposts in each side of the loom to keep the weaving from angling inward.

3. Thread the loom by tying the first notch, then pulling the yarn tautly across to the notch on the other side, around this notch, and back. Continue until you reach the end, wrap around the last notch, and knot.

4. Lay masking tape along each end to keep yarn in the notches.

5. Tie your first color yarn to the end warp and thread through a yarn needle. Continue to weave this color in and out in the areas for this only.

6. When two colors meet, you must dovetail them so that both colors wrap around the same warp thread where they meet, as shown.

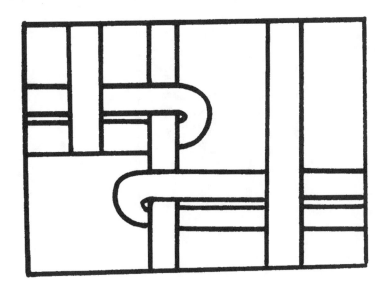

7. A rya knot can be included to make a fringe or carpet-looking row or area, as shown. Pull the knot tight and slide it down next to the other weaving. For the next row of rya knots, use one of the warp threads from the last knot above this and from the next wrap use one thread to wrap your knot around.

8. Alternating the threads will make all the knots stay in place better and will also make the finished piece look better.

9. To achieve curved shapes within the weaving, weave through a thread the regular way and then push it into the desired curve and fill in next to it with more lines of yarn until the desired space is filled in.

10. Lines can weave part way across, then turn and come back to achieve desired shapes in certain sections.

11. Empty negative space can be left.

12. A single or double warp cord can be wrapped tightly around and tied to achieve a spiraling effect, as shown.

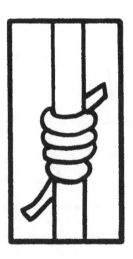

13. Weaving patterns can change, such as from over one–under one to over two–under three, to achieve a different look. Just remember to keep up the new pattern for several rows before changing, or the pattern will not emerge.

14. Beads can be added by threading them on at any time or by adding them to the warp threads at the beginning.

15. When finished, remove the masking tape and pull the yarn out of the notches.

16. Fringe can be tied to the bottom when finished.

17. The top loops can be laced through with a stick in order to hang your weaving.

Basket Weaving

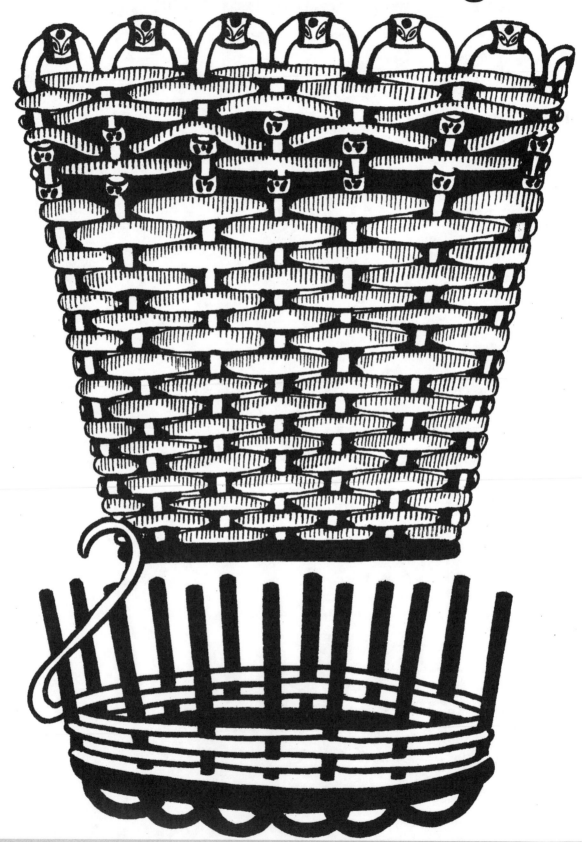

Basket Weaving

MATERIALS:

- **precut basket base (round or oval) with holes drilled**
- **#4 reed to be used for spokes**
- **#2 reed to be used for weaving**

Basket weaving has been done for thousands of years. In Egypt, many were found in tombs in the pyramids. At this time, baskets were used functionally—that is, to carry objects. Later, when they began to be painted they started to evolve into something more, and today many are appreciated for their beauty alone. The Native Indians and the Shakers in America became very skilled in their basket making. Baskets were woven of reeds, grasses, splints, straw, and cord.

DIRECTIONS:

1. Begin by placing the #4 and the #2 reeds in a container of water to soak. This will take about half an hour, so you may want to prepare this ahead of time.

2. Next, decide how tall you would like your basket to be. Whatever length you choose, add five inches to it. This is to allow extra length for the two parts of the reed that will be folded over.

3. Next, cut the #4 reeds to the desired length, and then insert them into the holes in the basket base. Let the reeds extend 2" below the base as shown.

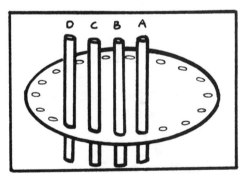

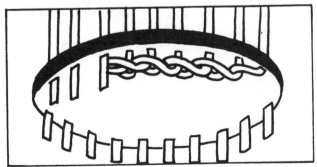

4. Starting with spoke A, weave the part that extends from the base around the outside of spoke B and secure it in front of spoke C. Next, weave spoke B around spoke C and secure it in front of spoke D. Follow the same procedure for the rest of the spokes.

5. Before you begin weaving the thin reed through the spokes, bend the spokes outward so that the sides of your basket will slant. Now you are ready to begin weaving the #2 reed in and out around the spokes. Make sure that the ends of each are inside the basket.

6. When you are finished weaving, you can complete your basket by taking the end of spoke A and looping it over and pushing the end down alongside spoke C. Push the end of spoke B down alongside spoke D. Continue this procedure until the edge is completed.

7. Upon completion, the baskets can be painted or preserved with a coat of shellac. If you wish to add beads, you can slide these onto the desired spokes at any point and then just continue to weave around them.

Crafts

LEVEL 4

Puppet on a String introduces a simple marionette with further work in costume design, characterization, and sewing. *Papier-Mâché Flu Bugs* reinforces the technique of papier-mâché with a wire armature, while *Fluorocarbon Foam Sculpture* explores carving as a new technique. *Creative Problem Solving* examines architecture using lines, as well as two-dimensional and three-dimensional forms to create fantasy structures for a specific purpose.

LEVEL 5

Gnomes involves further three-dimensional construction, while *Milk Jug Masks* gives continued work with characterization using various three-dimensional found objects in a relief form. *Butterfly Batik* introduces "batik" as an art form and also further work with detail. *Robots* involves creating a three-dimensional structure using scrap materials.

LEVEL 6

Balsa Wood Houses includes more advanced architectural concepts, presents a scale-plan drawing and further use with scrap materials, and the introduction of balsa wood. *Marionettes* involves more advanced marionettes and controls along with more advanced costume design and characterization. *Sand Casting* provides more advanced incised designing and the introduction of the new technique of sand casting. *Clone Soft Sculpture* continues sewing and costume design as well as presenting the technique of making dolls. *Creativity Kits* illustrates how unrelated scrap objects can be combined to create an art form. *Animation* introduces the use of a movie camera and the technique "animation," while *Zodiac Banners* presents the art form of banners and reinforces sewing techniques.

Puppet on a String

Butterfly Batik

Animation

Puppet on a String

Puppet on a String

MATERIALS:

- 1 pipe cleaner
- spools
- cardboard
- fabric
- sharp scissors
- lattice
- string
- paints and brushes
- needle and thread
- plaster-impregnated gauze
- small paper clips
- newspaper
- oaktag
- masking tape
- thin black marker
- yarn, feathers, and so forth
- staples

In such countries as Indonesia, Formosa, China, and Japan, the wide use of **puppets** goes back as far as the beginnings of recorded history. Puppets have been found in the ancient graves of Greece. In our own country, Native Indians used puppets in religious ceremonies long before the coming of the first European settlers. The Hindus once held a belief that each of their sacred puppets had lived with the gods.

DIRECTIONS:

1. Crumple a single sheet of newspaper into a ball shape and put tape around the ball so that it will hold its shape.

2. Tape the head to a spool, which forms its neck.

3. Use oaktag or newspaper to add features to the head, such as hats and beaks.

4. Twist a pipe cleaner into a small loop and tape it to the top of the head.

5. Layer and overlap gauze over the head and features, halfway down the neck, and around the pipe cleaner loop to hold securely. Let dry.

6. Paint the head. Let dry.

7. Lay out on appropriate piece of fabric and draw the body somewhat like the shape shown.

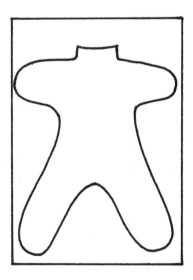

8. Cut out two pieces as patterns and sew them together using an overhand stitch close to the edge. Leave openings at the neck, ends of the arms, and ends of the legs.

9. Turn the costume.

10. Glue the neck spool into the neck opening of the costume and wrap with a piece of masking tape until dry.

11. Draw and cut out hand shapes from thin cardboard with an extension as shown. No more than four fingers are needed.

12. Draw and cut foot shapes from thin cardboard and glue onto a spool as shown.

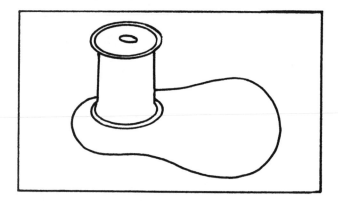

13. Layer gauze over the hands and feet halfway up the spool. Let dry.

14. Glue the hand extension and foot spool into the fabric openings and wrap masking tape around them until they dry.

15. Add yarn, feathers, and other details.

16. Cardboard wings for birds can replace the arms.

17. Cut out two pieces of lattice, each 6″ long. Cross the pieces, glue, and tape until dry.

18. Tie 2′ pieces of string at the end of each piece of lattice, glue, and tape in place.

19. Tie strings to the head pipe cleaner loop, wrists, and ankles as shown. Shorten the strings as necessary to achieve a straight string from the control to the puppet in each area.

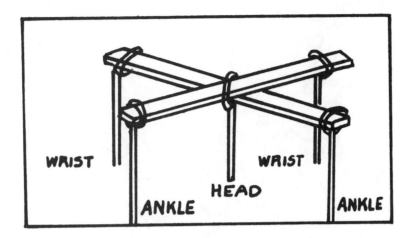

Papier-Mâché Flu Bugs

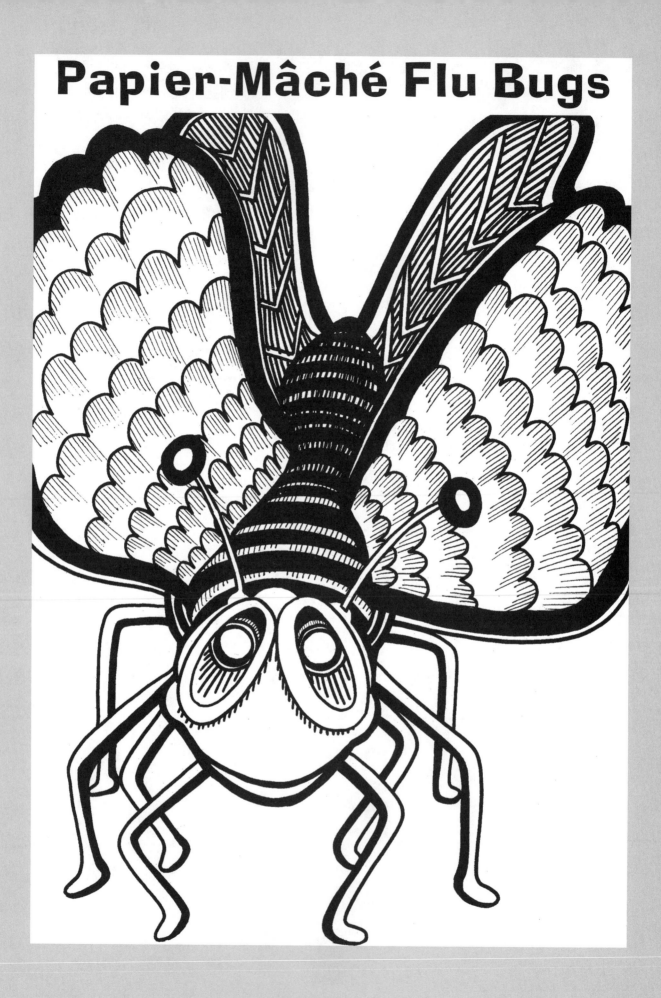

Papier-Mâché Flu Bugs

MATERIALS:

- **flexible aluminum wire**
- **newspaper**
- **masking tape**
- **wire cutter**
- **tempera paints and brushes**
- **tissue paper**
- **scissors**
- **pipe cleaners**
- **oaktag**
- **12" x 18" paper**
- **pencil and eraser**
- **acrylic polymer medium**
- **plaster-impregnated gauze**

Papier-mâché is a substance made of pulped paper or paper mixed with glue or layers of paper glued and pressed together, which are molded when moist and which become hard and strong when dry. The Chinese were the first to use this method, and they used it to create strong furniture.

DIRECTIONS:

1. Draw your idea of a horrible flu bug. Make it menacing.

2. Lay out two sheets of newspaper on top of each other and fold them in half. Fold the paper in half again.

3. Cut a piece of wire about 3" longer than the length of the paper and lay it inside the paper. Roll the wire up inside the paper.

4. Bend another piece of wire in one of the shapes shown for one wing.

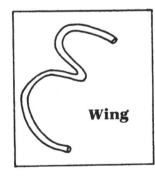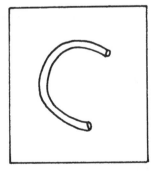

Wing

5. Do the same for the other wing.

6. Roll up newspaper to make a body, as shown.

7. Attach wings onto the body with tape.

8. Wings can be your idea or like the one shown.

9. The body can be bent, as shown.

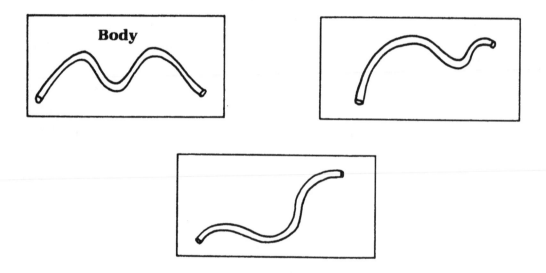

10. Wad a piece of newspaper into a ball and tape to hold.

11. Part of the head can be pushed in to form a mouth and teeth, and a tongue can be added.

12. Tape a pipe cleaner—cut in half—onto the head for antennae.

13. Bulging eyes, other features, bumps on the body, and wings can be added with a wad of newspaper or oaktag cut in a desired shape.

14. Pipe cleaner legs can also be added.

15. The wings can be made of flat sheets of newspaper cut to fit, laid on the frame, and taped to hold.

16. Cover the entire form, except for the antennae, with plaster-impregnated gauze. Let dry.

17. Paint with tempera, including patterns and designs.

18. Coat with a layer of acrylic polymer medium.

Fluorocarbon Foam Sculpture

Fluorocarbon Foam Sculpture

MATERIALS:

- fluorocarbon foam blocks
- simple carving tools like spoons, craft sticks, clay modeling tools
- shallow box (to collect the carvings)
- 12" x 18" manila paper
- pencil and eraser
- ruler and scissors
- rough and medium sand paper

Sculpture is an art form that is three-dimensional. It has height, width, and depth. When making sculpture, the artist must remember to look at all sides while working because they are all important.

DIRECTIONS:

1. Make a drawing on a piece of 12" x 18" manila paper of what you want to carve.

2. Measure the sides of the block and cut three papers to these sizes.

3. Transfer this preliminary drawing to the three papers with a different view on each—front, side, and back, as shown.

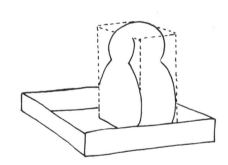

4. Maker sure each drawing touches all edges of the paper. Cut out each.

5. Lay drawing on its appropriate side and draw around it into the foam block.

6. Place the block in a box to do the carving.

7. Next, round out the forms by turning the block constantly as you go.

8. Incise the edge of shapes to emphasize parts or features you want to bring out.

9. First use rough and then medium sandpaper to finish.

Creative Problem Solving

Creative Problem Solving

MATERIALS:

- **toothpicks**
- **egg cartons**
- **Styrofoam sheets**
- **scissors**
- **masking tape**
- **glue**
- **slides or photos of various architecture**

To be **creative** means to use one's own original ideas or imagination.

DIRECTIONS:

1. Look at slides or photos of various architecture, including fantasy architecture from space and adventure movies or stories.

2. Architectural design is made up of line, and two-dimensional and three-dimensional forms.

3. Construct three buildings, each using only one of the above elements as its basis.

4. In addition, make one of each of these buildings that is appropriate for the following movies:
   - A story about fairies and angels who live in a beautiful place.
   - A story about evil creatures on another planet who capture all who land on their planet.
   - A story about some strong, friendly giants who welcome all who enter their kingdom.

Gnomes

Gnomes

MATERIALS:

- **empty fruit juice can**
- **construction-paper cone**
- **scissors**
- **felt and pipe cleaner**
- **fiberfill stuffing, cotton, or white fur**
- **newspaper**
- **tempera paints and brushes**
- **medium-sized Styrofoam ball**
- **cardboard**
- **pom-pom**
- **masking tape**
- **white glue**

A **gnome** is one of a species of small beings fabled to inhabit the interior of the Earth and to act as guardian of its treasures. It is usually thought of as a shriveled little old man or a troll.

DIRECTIONS:

1. Take one empty fruit juice can and attach a Styrofoam ball to the top with glue.

2. Model the face by using thin strips of newspaper dipped in watered-down white glue.

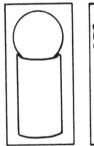

3. A beard can be made by attaching fiberfill or cotton to the face with white glue. You can also use some for eyebrows or for hair.

4. Next, attach a cone (the cardboard type used to support spools of yarn are an ideal size) or create one from construction paper by cutting out a shape like this. Twist it into a cone and glue the seam.

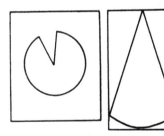

5. Next, paint the face and cut out felt eyes and cheeks. If so desired, a pom-pom can be used for a nose.

6. The next step is to cover the can with felt to create the clothing. Felt-covered cardboard feet can be taped to the bottom of the can. Extended arms can be added by piercing the sides of the can and running a pipe cleaner through the center, which can later be covered with felt.

Milk Jug Masks

Milk Jug Masks

MATERIALS:

- empty, plastic gallon container (milk, bleach, and so forth)
- plaster-impregnated gauze
- old scissors and craft knife
- large plastic bowls and water
- tempera paints and brushes
- junk items, such as cardboard tubes, egg cartons, cans, feathers, oatmeal box, salt box, toothpaste box
- masking tape
- slides or photos of historical masks

DIRECTIONS:

1. View slides or photos of historical masks.

2. Cut the plastic container in half so that the handle will become the base for the nose on your mask. (See the illustration.) Cut off the bottom of the container so that you are left with a curved, face-size piece for the mask.

3. Attach various scrap items to your mask with masking tape to create eyes, nose, mouth, ears, eyebrows, teeth, cheeks, hat, or whatever is desired. Make sure that the item stands out far enough in relief so that even when it is covered with plaster-impregnated gauze, the item is still prominent.

4. Scrap objects can be cut in various ways to change their shape.

5. Eyes can be cut through the bottle with a craft knife, if desired.

6. Cut the gauze with old scissors, then dip the gauze into plastic bowls of warm water. Next, layer the gauze in an overlapping fashion to cover all the features and plastic of the bottle that will be the face. No gauze should cover the back of the mask.

7. Try to make the layering as smooth as possible. Rub the gauze with your fingers to smooth the surface and release plaster to fill in the holes in the gauze.

8. After drying, tempera can be used to add color.

9. Feathers, fake fur, yarn, pipe cleaners, raffia, and so forth may also be added.

10. After large painted areas are completed and dried, patterns can be added with a smaller brush in contrasting colors.

11. When dry, scissors can be used to cut out the back and bottom and to make holes in each side to wear the mask or to hang it using string.

Butterfly Batik

Butterfly Batik

MATERIALS:

- washed, bleached muslin
- pencil and eraser
- water-soluble, bottled wax medium
- stiff narrow brushes
- cold-water dyes and cold water
- brushes

- 12" x 16" paper
- vinegar
- plastic bowls
- newspaper
- iron (use with adult supervision)

Batik is an Indonesian word that describes a form of resist printing obtained when hot wax, an effective resistant to dye, is applied to the fabric. Fine patterns are often made by using a tjanting, a tool for applying hot wax. When the fabric is dyed, only the unwaxed areas of the cloth take the color. Dyeing is carried out in cool water to prevent the wax from melting.

DIRECTIONS:

1. Draw a simple butterfly shape to fill the paper.
2. Add simple designs in one wing. Repeat the same designs in reverse, on the opposite wing.
3. Copy the drawing on the muslin in a light pencil line.
4. Trace over the lines with the wax solution to which you have mixed enough water so that it can be easily applied, yet it can penetrate and cover the cloth. Let dry.
5. Mix the cold-water dyes in plastic bowls.
6. Using one color for the background and many colors for the inside of the butterfly, brush on the dyes.
7. Let dry.
8. Place the muslin on a thick pad of newspaper with one piece of newsprint on top.
9. Iron over the newsprint and keep changing to a new sheet of the newsprint until all the wax is gone.
10. Wax over the entire cloth with a wide brush.
11. Let dry completely and crinkle the cloth into a ball.
12. Lay flat and paint a strong solution of black dye over the entire cloth.
13. Again, iron out the wax.
14. Finish with a cold-water bath with vinegar to fix the dye and let dry.

Copper Foil Jewelry

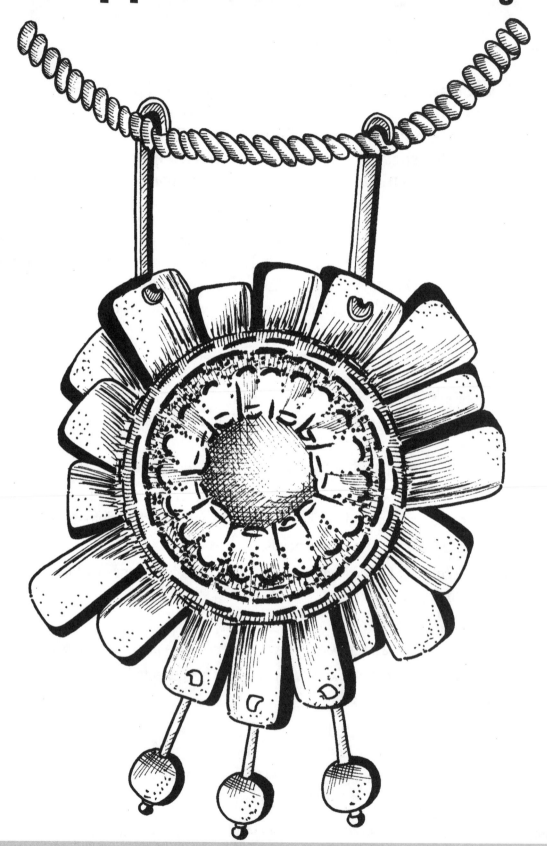

Copper Foil Jewelry

MATERIALS:

- paper and pencil
- 36-gauge copper
- scissors
- craft knives
- metal shears
- needle-nose pliers
- 14-, 16-, or 18-gauge copper wire or galvanized iron wire (stovepipe)
- rawhide strings
- various found objects for stamping
- wooden stick
- beads, twigs, stone, leather

- jeweler's findings (pin backs, clips, links and catches)
- epoxy
- wire cutters
- ball-pin hammer
- steel block
- liver of sulphur
- fine-grade steel wool
- candle in a secure holder
- acrylics
- slides or photos of jewelry

DIRECTIONS:

1. View slides or photos of historical and contemporary jewelry.

2. View slides of macrocosmic sections of objects from nature and use the repetition you see to draw pencil designs or preliminary sketches for your finished jewelry. Simplify the basic shapes of birds, fish, and animals.

3. Cut your basic shape or shapes out of the copper with the metal shears.

4. Think of ways you can shape the metal to create interest. You might: (1) cut an opening within a shape; (2) cut a second shape to glue on top of the first shape; (3) cut a shape and texture the surface by hammering (use a ball-pin hammer and steel block).

5. Design each shape by the repoussé technique on the metal and connect with rings where necessary.

6. Cut a piece of wire between 12" and 18" long and coil it around a pencil or a small dowel. After removing it from the pencil, stretch it. Coil another piece of wire (similar to the way a rope would be coiled) flat on a table. Pull it out from the center.

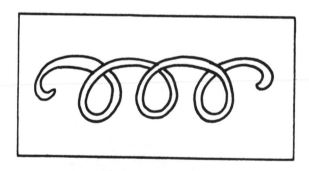

7. Think of how you can convert forms such as these into jewelry. Try other methods for coiling, bending, and twisting wire.

8. How could a series of similarly coiled wire forms be combined into a necklace? Would colorful beads or chunks of stone enhance the design?

9. Flatten a piece of 16-gauge copper wire by hammering it on the steel block. Could you coil this or part of it for your design?

10. If you plan to develop an opening (negative space) within the metal shape, drill a hole at that point, insert scissors, and cut away with the points.

11. Metal pieces or jeweler's findings may be joined with epoxy.

12. Remember, the copper foil can be easily cut with scissors, or torn, rolled, folded, or crumpled.

13. Pieces can be joined by rawhide lacing or wire.

14. You can use the repoussé technique of burnishing with a wooden spoon or stick and/or stamping with any hard object. Texture rubbings can be added for surface texture.

15. Outside edges may be folded over and burnished to provide a more rigid and less fragile piece.

16. A patina is achieved by submerging or brushing a solution of liver of sulphur on the surface, then polishing with a fine grade of steel wool to highlight the raised surface.

17. Heat applied to the foil will give a range of varying colors from red to yellow to green and blue. Test on a scrap piece first by holding over a candle.

18. Subtle colors of acrylics painted on the foil and wiped off immediately will give an interesting accent.

Robots

Robots

MATERIALS:

- **boxes of all shapes and sizes**
- **scrap machine parts**
- **foil**
- **glue**
- **paint and brushes**
- **masking tape**
- **lights, pipes, hoses, wire**
- **aluminum foil**

DIRECTIONS:

1. **a.** Decide upon a task or tasks you want your robot to perform. How will you simulate this?

   b. Assemble boxes by gluing and holding them in place with masking tape as they dry. These will form the basic body shape of your robot.

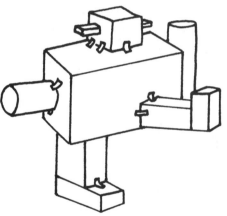

2. Add various scrap materials to construct arms and legs or wheels so the robot can stand or move.

3. Add lights if desired.

4. Add slots for questions, or knobs, or dials.

5. You might cut a hole to expose "machine parts"— which you have glued or wired inside the robot's body.

6. When the construction is complete, paint or cover parts with aluminum foil.

7. You should include a set of directions in order to show how your robot will perform his or her assigned task.

Balsa Wood Houses

1st FLOOR

Bath

Play Room

Bedroom

2nd FLOOR

Kitchen

Living Room

Master Bedroom

Balsa Wood Houses

MATERIALS:

- pencil and eraser
- 12" x 18" paper
- balsa wood and craft knife
- water-soluble wood glue
- plaster-impregnated gauze

- straight pins
- masking tape
- rulers
- stain or paint
- newspaper

- 18" x 24" newsboard
- brushes
- dowels, other scrap materials
- wooden dowels

DIRECTIONS:

1. Design and draw the outside elevation and inside floor plan for a vacation house for the year 2100 for a family of four with no more than seven rooms.

2. Indicate on your paper where you want the house to be built. Take this into consideration when deciding the type of energy to be used in your house, windows, transportation to the house, and so forth.

3. On a board, approximately 18" x 24", draw your floor plan.

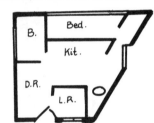

4. If your house is on irregular ground, build this up first by using crushed wads of newspaper covered with plaster-impregnated gauze.

5. Houses may be on stilts made of wooden dowels.

6. Using balsa wood pieces measuring 3" x ¹⁄₁₆" x 24", cut the wood so that between 1" and 1 ½" equals one floor wall. Remember to cut out the windows before gluing up the walls on the base.

7. The outside doors should be drawn on and the inside walls cut out.

8. All outside walls should be constructed before the inside walls.

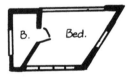

9. The roof should be constructed so that at least part of it can be removed to view the inside of the house.

10. Other scrap materials, such as the bottoms of two-liter soda bottles for skylights, and other effects such as acetate for "glass" can be used.

11. When complete, stain or paint your house.

12. Trees or bushes from hobby train stores can be glued on the board, as can sand for beaches, fake grass, and painted lakes or oceans.

13. Possible ideas could be a house on an island, one underwater, one underground, heliports on roofs, computer rooms, robot servants, and so forth.

Marionettes

Marionettes

MATERIALS:

- masking tape
- plaster-impregnated gauze
- empty plastic two-liter soda bottle
- craft knife
- muslin
- 1" wood for feet
- ⅜" dowel
- cardboard

- needle and thread
- felt, material, yarn
- tongue depressor, lattice strips
- screw eyes
- nylon fishing line
- fiberfill stuffing
- newspaper, cardboard

DIRECTIONS:

1. Sketch your favorite character.

2. Wrap single sheets of newspaper over each other to form a ball and fasten with tape to the top of the bottle. Add features to your head with cardboard or rolled newspaper.

3. Cut four holes in the bottle for arms and legs.

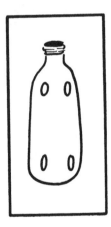

4. Smoothly cover the head and neck with plaster-saturated gauze. Overlap the gauze onto the bottle in order to secure the head.

5. Sew ⅝" seam on two pieces of muslin that have been cut 3" x 20" to be used as arms and legs. Turn the inside out.

6. Push the muslin pieces through the holes and stuff with fiberfill; tie, as shown, at the joints.

7. Cut two wooden feet 1" x 2 ½" and drill a hole in each so that you can insert a ⅜" x 3" dowel into each. Secure these with white glue.

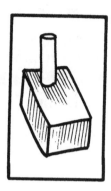

8. Cut out two cardboard hands and then cover each with felt. When they are dry, glue one inside each arm.

9. Paint the head, arms, legs, feet, and hands if you wish. Add yarn or fake fur for hair.

10. Use felt or other materials to construct a costume if one is needed. Your costume can be sewn or glued together.

11. Next, construct your controls using strips of lattice and a tongue depressor. If possible, drill holes where shown. Overlap strips of wood and then glue them together.

12. The last step is stringing, and this requires that a screw eye be hammered into the head so that the marionette can hang from the controls. Next, use a needle and fishing twine to join the knees and hands to the controls, as shown.

Sand Casting

Sand Casting

MATERIALS:

- aluminum pie or baking tin
- plaster of Paris
- variety of interesting large objects and tools, such as shells, gears, wheels, kitchen gadgets, and sticks

- soft brush
- plastic bucket
- pipe cleaner

DIRECTIONS:

1. Pack clean, moist sand in a pie or baking tin.

2. Impress a design or push objects into the sand and lift out to leave an impression.

3. With your hands, mix plaster of Paris into a plastic bucket that already has some water in it by slowly adding some of the plaster powder until the mixture has the consistency of heavy cream.

4. Carefully pour the plaster over the sand and into the impressions. Embed a bent pipe cleaner to use as a hanger.

5. When the plaster is fully set, loosen by gently bending the aluminum pan.

6. Brush off loose sand with a soft brush, but leave the sandy surface that is embedded in the plaster.

7. Sand casting will not reproduce the minute details that a clay casting will.

8. Quick, bold designs work best.

Clone Soft Sculpture

Clone Soft Sculpture

MATERIALS:

- felt
- fabric
- yarn
- sharp scissors
- craft or fabric glue
- polyester fiberfill
- thread and needle
- straight pins
- nylons and socks
- costume jewelry
- wigs
- hairpieces
- furs
- sequins
- buttons
- collars and ties
- artificial flowers
- glasses
- 18" x 24" manila paper

A **clone** is the exact duplicate of another living thing.

DIRECTIONS:

1. Make a list of all your personality traits. Include a list of things you love, things you dislike, what makes you excited or happy, what makes you sad, what hobbies you have, and what sports you like.

2. On a piece of 18" x 24" manila paper, draw a simple human figure, perhaps in a position you often take.

3. Pin this to a folded piece of felt.

4. Sew a blanket stitch all the way around the figure.

5. There are also three other stuffed people shapes you could make: (1) The single-shaped doll contains head, arms, trunk, and legs in one shape; parts are not added separately. (2) The arch-shape doll contains the head and the body; the arms and legs are added separately. (3) The stocking doll is created from old nylons, stuffed, stitched, and formed into a head, body, arms, and legs.

6. For the single-shape and arch-shape doll, the directions include making a paper pattern, pinning it to doubled cloth, cutting it out, and sewing the two parts together. Leave a hole for the stuffing. The stocking doll requires that you wrap and tie a section of nylon stocking around a head-shaped ball of stuffing.

7. Your pattern should not be too skinny or too complicated, or it will be impossible to sew and stuff. With the arch-shape doll, the pattern is no problem—it's just a big arch shape. The stocking doll needs no pattern at all.

8. Remember to place the pattern on the edge of the fabric, not in the center.

9. Pin the fronts and backs. Choose the running stitch, overcast, or blanket stitch. See the illustrations below.

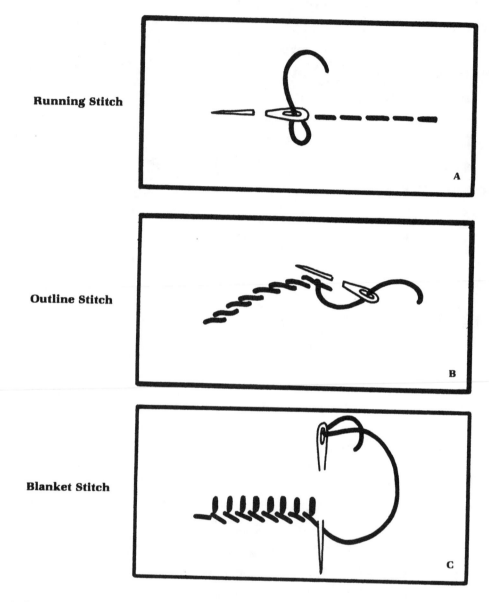

Running Stitch — A

Outline Stitch — B

Blanket Stitch — C

10. Stitch around the outside edge of your doll and remember to leave an opening for the stuffing.

11. If you have used a running stitch, you may wish to turn your doll inside out after stitching.

12. With a stocking doll, once you have formed and tied a stocking head, begin a nose by making small stitches through the nylon and the stuffing and pulling them tight.

13. Experiment with ways to form eyes, lips, and cheeks with a stocking doll. Stitch arms, legs, and bodies together.

14. Clothes can be sewn or glued onto the doll.

15. Optional finishing touches such as hair, eyelashes, and fingernails are glued to the outside of the clone.

16. Items may be made and added to the clone to make them look more like you, that is, a book, a baseball bat, a science beaker, riding boots, and so forth.

17. Remember you are making a clone—an exact duplicate of you—so *always* keep this in mind when forming the features, the color and style of the hair, the type of clothes, and props.

Creativity Kits

Creativity Kits

MATERIALS:

- 2 pipe cleaners
- 2 craft sticks
- 2 paper clips
- 2 plastic straws
- 2 toothpicks
- 2 brass paper fasteners
- 2 sheets 9" x 12" colored or white paper
- 1 sheet 9" x 12" oaktag
- scissors
- glue
- pencil and eraser
- markers
- string
- stapler

DIRECTIONS:

1. Using *all* of the materials given above, construct a three-dimensional recognizable object. Try to stretch your imagination to make something really different.

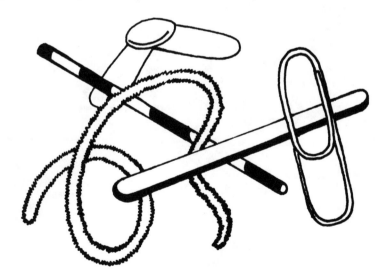

2. You may also use standard art supplies, such as scissors, glue, pencil, and eraser.

3. Try to avoid the obvious.

Animation

Animation

MATERIALS:

- **super 8 mm camera with a macrozoom lens and a single frame adjustment (a video camera would be an alternative choice)**
- **extra long cable release**
- **editor and splicer (optional)**
- **splicing tapes**
- **reels**
- **plasticene**
- **pencil and eraser**
- **paint and brushes and glue**
- **pieces of 18" x 24" butcher paper**
- **3 or 4 pieces of 18" x 24" illustration board**
- **2 reflector floodlights of 300 watts and clamps or poles in porcelain sockets**
- **cassette recorder**

DIRECTIONS:

1. Write an original short story using characters that are inventive and creative. Include conversation and sound effects.

2. Stress exaggerated action and descriptive words.

3. Draw and paint scenery on butcher paper and glue it onto a piece of illustration board.

4. Mold your characters and props out of plasticene and remember to keep them in proportion to an area that measures 18" x 24".

5. Different heads can be made for the characters to interchange so that different facial expressions can be shown.

6. Colors of characters must be in contrast to the scenery so that they can be seen.

7. Use a simple frame-cable release to shoot two frames, then move an arm, leg, and/or head of your character *slightly*. Shoot another two frames or clicks with the cable release.

8. Shoot every scene in sequence to avoid as much editing and splicing as possible. (Directions are easy and come with the editor.)

9. Remember that 24 frames = 1 second of the movie—so your movements or changes between every two frames must be small.

10. Two frames per move will give you fairly smooth action when the film is projected.

11. You can write conversation on cardboard and insert these in between the action, or you can view the film when it is finished and tape the voices and sound effects on a cassette.

Zodiac Banners

Zodiac Banners

MATERIALS:

- butcher paper
- drawing paper
- pencil and eraser
- sharp scissors
- felt and fabric
- fabric or craft glue
- markers
- burlap
- large tapestry needles
- rug, knitting, and brill yarns
- embroidery paint and brushes
- various found objects including mirrors, sequins, lace, rickrack, braid, trims, roving, and so forth
- wooden dowels

DIRECTIONS:

1. Banners came into use in the Middle Ages and were carried into battles to show certain groups or rulers. Later, business people used them in front of their shops for advertising. Banners are used today to decorate, advertise, and identify.

2. Using the zodiac symbol for your birth month, draw an idea for a banner and use the symbol as the central idea. Include objects around it showing something about you, your characteristics, and the things you enjoy. Perhaps you could show a turtle because everything you do, you do slowly and carefully. Or, you could show a book because you love to read.

3. You might include your favorite foods.

4. Various objects should be organized in groups or sections and separated by lines, designs, or colors into certain areas.

5. When your sketch is organized, transfer it to butcher paper and outline objects in black marker.

6. Select a color of burlap and cut out the desired size.

7. Edges should be either fringed or trimmed with ready-made fringe.

8. Tops should be turned over and stitched down to allow for the dowel sticks.

9. Roving should be braided and attached to each end of the stick.

10. Use objects cut from the butcher paper to trace around the felt or fabric. Cut the objects out and glue them into place.

11. Large needles and yarns can be used to add stitchery where desired.

12. A decorative quality can be achieved by using junk jewelry, feathers, mirrors, plastic eyes, sticks, and buttons.

13. Embroidery paint can be used for smaller details and outlines.

NOTES

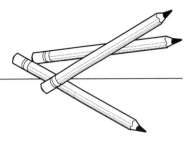

NOTES

NOTES

NOTES

NOTES

NOTES